THE COPING WITH DEPRESSION COURSE

A Psychoeducational Intervention for Unipolar Depression

Peter M. Lewinsohn
David O. Antonuccio
Julia Steinmetz Breckenridge
Linda Teri

Castalia Publishing Company
P.O. Box 1587
Eugene, OR 97440

ISBN 0-916154-11-4

Printed in the United States of America

Editorial and Production Credits:
    Editor-in-Chief: Scot G. Patterson
    Copy Editor: Cheryl Brunette
    Editor's Assistant: Jina LaMear
    Editor's Assistant: Jody Kishpaugh
    Typesetting and Layout: John Macioce

Contents

Preface

This book has been written to provide a detailed description of a research-based treatment program that has been developed for unipolar depression. The treatment approach is based on a group format, and a course entitled "Coping with Depression" is the vehicle for therapy. The course was first offered in 1979 through the Depression Research Unit at the University of Oregon. Since then, over three hundred individuals have enrolled in the course. The efficacy of the course has been evaluated in a number of studies, and additional research is in progress. The completed studies show quite clearly that when evaluated as a group, the participants in this course show marked improvement in their depression level, and that these changes are maintained for at least six months after treatment. Research is currently under way to determine the impact of treatment after a three-year follow-up period. These treatment successes have prompted us to refine our training manual for dissemination to practitioners in other settings.

Our work with depression began in 1965 at the University of Oregon when the senior author, as a result of his teaching, found that there was very little empirical knowledge about the psychosocial factors associated with depression. A review of the literature suggested that there were no treatment outcome studies to build upon. Professional thinking at the time was focused on psychoanalytic formulations, even though it was acknowledged that the treatment methods based on these formulations were ineffective in alleviating depression. In an attempt to help fill this void, Lewinsohn and his colleagues began a series of behaviorally oriented clinical research studies that had the dual function of testing hypotheses about the psychosocial antecedents for depression as well as developing and testing treatment methods. These studies were part of a larger movement in which innovative behavioral approaches to a variety of clinical problems were beginning to appear in the literature. However, behavioral researchers had only recently begun to study the phenomenon of depression. The first behaviorally oriented single-case studies did not appear in the literature until the late 1960s, and it was not until 1973 that the first group-design studies were reported. Since 1973, over forty outcome studies of behavioral treatments of depression have appeared in the literature. Thus, the systematic investigation of depression within a behavioral framework is a very recent phenomenon.

It became clear as our work progressed that a variety of structured behavioral and cognitive therapies were effective in ameliorating depression. The components of our treatment program were derived from our own research and clinical contacts as well as from a rapidly expanding body of literature. The parts of the program that had been shown to be most effective were retained, while those that were least helpful were dropped or substantially revised. Finally, after more than a decade of research and clinical work, the book *Control Your Depression* was written in 1978 by Lewinsohn, Muñoz, Youngren, and Zeiss. The purpose of that book was to provide a multi-component approach emphasizing general self-help skills for depressed individuals. The book focused on four common problem areas: 1) excessive anxiety or tension, 2) a low rate of pleasant activities, 3) conflicted social interactions, and 4) negative thinking. *Control Your Depression* offered readers direct instruction on how to enhance their skills in these areas. However, when we wrote *Control Your Depression* in 1978 we were aware that handing the book to depressed individuals and expecting them to do all the work by themselves would not be sufficient; some amount of support, encouragement, clarification, and assistance would be required for most people to make use of these skills in their daily lives. The Coping with Depression course was developed to serve this supportive function.

Our efforts gained momentum in the fall of 1978 when Dr. Arthur Ulene asked us to use *Control Your Depression* with a group of depressed individuals recruited by his staff for an educational television program he was producing for NBC. With considerable anxiety we accepted the challenge. In a rented meeting room in San Francisco, each of the authors of *Control Your Depression* led two sessions in front of the TV cameras. In spite of (or perhaps because of) the extraordinary circumstances, the first

Coping with Depression course went extremely well.

After returning to Eugene we were highly motivated to develop the group format more systematically. The first study was conducted by Dr. Peter Lewinsohn and Dr. Richard Brown. Most of the treatment format that is described in this book was developed while leading the groups that participated in that first study. Drs. Julia Steinmetz and David Antonuccio, who had participated as instructors in the first study, played the major role in the second study in which the class protocol became more systematized and many of the procedures for training instructors were consolidated.

The Coping with Depression Course seemed to address most of the problems experienced by depressed individuals. Our research indicated that 80% were nondepressed after taking the course. Perhaps even more of the participants found it to be a meaningful and valuable experience. Because it could be offered in groups, it was clearly a cost-effective treatment. We have also found that it has been relatively easy to train course instructors (therapists). However, we want to emphasize that our instructors have been professional psychologists and advanced graduate students in clinical and counseling psychology who have had extensive clinical experience. All of these instructors were provided with systematic and concentrated training based on a very structured treatment manual that was the predecessor of this book (Steinmetz, Antonuccio, Bond, McKay, Brown, & Lewinsohn, 1979). They were also provided with close ongoing clinical supervision (the procedures used for training instructors are discussed in Chapter 3).

The approach described in this book has a definite structure that dictates a large part of the agenda for each of the treatment sessions. If psychotherapeutic approaches were placed along a continuum where one pole represents the therapies in which the client determines the agenda for each session (e.g., nondirective therapy), and the other pole represents the therapies in which the therapist determines the agenda (e.g., relaxation training), then our Coping with Depression course approach lies near the latter pole. Nevertheless, there is nothing mechanical about conducting these courses. Each group is different and poses a unique set of challenges. There is considerable room for creativity, imaginativeness, and clinical skill.

Intended Audience

The intended audience for this book is mental health professionals who want to learn a new approach for working with depressed individuals. This book is designed to be used by clinicians who already have basic clinical skills (see Chapter 3) and at least some experience in teaching a class or leading a therapy group. In addition, readers should have some familiarity with behavioral and cognitive approaches to psychological treatment. Individuals who are not familiar with these approaches should read *Social Learning Theory* by Bandura (1977) for an introduction to the basic theory. Since many sections of this book, especially Chapter 6, are unintelligible without having read *Control Your Depression,* readers are also urged to become thoroughly familiar with *Control Your Depression* before attempting to use this book.

We have tried to describe the Coping with Depression course in a pragmatic and understandable manner for the practitioner or practitioner-in-training. At the same time, the theoretical and empirical foundations upon which this approach is based are presented. Although no written text can take the place of experiential learning, it is hoped that this book can bridge the gap between the on-line practitioner wanting a "how-to" approach, and the plethora of research studies available in the scholarly journals today.

This book is the result of our research and clinical contacts with depressed individuals. As such, the content represents a dynamic process directed toward designing a program that is increasingly effective in alleviating depression. To facilitate our efforts in these directions, we would like to encourage those who read this book to give us feedback on their experiences in offering the Coping with Depression course. Appendix 1.1 has been included to provide an opportunity to communicate your suggestions for ways to improve the course.

Organization of the Book

There are four major sections of this book. The first section (Chapters 1 & 2) provides background information and an introduction to the theoretical underpinnings of the Coping with Depression course. The second section (Chapters 3, 4, & 5) outlines the preliminary steps for offering the course. Chapter 3 summarizes the criteria for selecting instructors and the procedures for training them to be effective course leaders. Chapter 4 suggests strategies for making the course known in the community. Media advertising and other community outreach procedures are covered in detail; issues relating to ethical considerations in advertising are also included. In Chapter 5, intake assessment procedures and criteria for selecting participants are outlined. The third section (Chapters 6 & 7) presents the curriculum for the Coping with Depression course and proposes solutions for common problems with participants. Chapter 6 is the heart of the book in that it provides a description of the 12 sessions that make up the course. The material is presented in a comprehensive lecture format that covers the components of the course in detail. Chapter 7 includes methods for dealing with participants who dominate class discussions (i.e., "Monopolizers") and techniques for motivating participants who are withdrawn or underinvolved (i.e., "Nonparticipators"). The fourth section (Chapters 8, 9, & 10) is concerned with issues relating to assessment and research. In Chapter 8, an outline of assessment procedures is offered. Chapter 9 summarizes the research findings regarding the effectiveness of the course in alleviating depression. Chapter 10 proposes areas for future research and other possible applications for the Coping with Depression course format.

Acknowledgments

There are many individuals who have made valuable contributions to the development of the approach described in this book and to the preparation of the manuscript. The authors wish to express their appreciation to Carolyn Alexander for her diligent and excellent work in making the final revisions and for taking care of many of the required details; Teal Korn for her careful work in typing the many original drafts; Scot Patterson for being such a good and helpful editor; and to the many former graduate students of the University of Oregon's doctoral program in Clinical Psychology for their creativity and enthusiasm. Specifically we would like to mention Chris Amenson, Meg Bond, Richard Brown, Teresa Chamberlin, Joseph Flippo, Linda Gonzales, Sally Grosscup, Don Killian, Julian Libet, Garth McKay, Douglas MacPhillamy, Ricardo Muñoz, John Robinson, Maria Saenz, Victor Sanchez, David Shaw, Mark Tilson, Mary Ann Youngren, and Antonette Zeiss.

Chapter 1

Introduction

Depression is a relatively common problem that is experienced by clinical and nonclinical populations alike. It is a particularly debilitating disorder that affects—and in turn is affected by—the daily functioning of the individual. Episodes of depression can impair work performance, damage social interactions, hamper family relations, and undermine the individual's feelings of self-worth. The prevalence of depression and the fact that it is particularly disabling highlight the need for a cost-effective treatment for depression.

Defining the Problem

In breaking away from psychoanalytic formulations of depression, the first task for behaviorally oriented researchers was to empirically delineate a set of depressive behaviors. This was accomplished by a series of descriptive studies of clinically depressed individuals which used symptom ratings to establish the components of the depression syndrome (e.g., Grinker, Miller, Sabshin, Nunn, & Nunnally, 1961). The list of symptoms was then reduced to a number of clusters through factor analysis. It is reassuring to note that considerable agreement has been demonstrated across descriptive studies as to the components of the depression syndrome (Lewinsohn, Teri, & Hoberman, 1983). These factor-analytic studies suggest that the symp-

1

toms of depression can be divided into six general categories: dysphoria, reduced rate of behavior, social-interactional problems, guilt, material burden, and somatic complaints. These categories represent distinct symptom clusters which make it possible to define depression operationally.

The Symptoms of Depression

Dysphoria. The most pervasive symptom of depression is a dysphoric state of feeling sad or blue. When asked to verbalize how they feel, depressed individuals will often describe their dysphoria using expressions such as "worthless," "helpless," "pessimistic," and "down." During episodes of depression they may feel uncertain about their intelligence and competence at work, even though an objective appraisal of their skills may not support their assertions. For depressed individuals the future holds nothing but gloomy prospects and there is nothing to look forward to.

Reduced Rate of Behavior. The majority of seriously depressed individuals exhibit an overall reduction in activity level. While the occurrence of some covert behaviors such as negative cognitions may increase dramatically, it has been shown that during episodes of depression individuals *do* considerably less than when they are not depressed. A typical day for a depressed patient may consist largely of passive solitary activities such as watching television or sleeping. Going to work or performing daily household chores may seem increasingly effortful, and in some of the more extreme cases these tasks may be neglected altogether. Activities and hobbies that were once pleasurable may become arduous and unenjoyable.

Social-Interactional Problems. Many depressed individuals express a variety of concerns about their interpersonal relationships. For many depressed patients, marital problems are a source of unhappiness and distress. Others may feel anxious and uncomfortable in social situations. Some depressed patients also express concern about their passivity and tendency to be socially withdrawn. These patients may feel conflicted about their relationships with other people. For example, they may complain about feeling lonely yet express little interest in being with others.

Guilt. It is fairly common for depressed individuals to express feelings of guilt. When asked to describe the reason for their guilt, some individuals will suggest that they are unable to satisfy specific family responsibilities or perform adequately at work. These persons tend to view themselves as being a burden to others. For other depressed individuals the guilt feelings may be more diffuse, and patients will report that they deserve to be punished for something that they have done.

Material Burden. Some patients have a tendency to blame their depressed moods upon external circumstances such as financial difficulty or a

2

conflict with their employer. These individuals frequently assert that excessive demands are being placed upon them by their families or employers; they believe that their mood would be improved if these material problems could be resolved. In general, they do not see themselves as being responsible for their problems.

Somatic Complaints. Most depressed individuals seeking professional help will describe a number of somatic complaints. One of the most common symptoms of depression is sleep disturbance; difficulty in falling asleep, restless sleep, and early morning wakening are often reported. Another common somatic symptom is a loss of appetite leading to weight loss. Patients report not enjoying their meals and find themselves not eating on a regular basis. Other frequent symptoms of depression include chronic fatigue, headaches, loss of sex drive, and upper gastrointestinal problems. It is important, however, particularly when working with the elderly, to rule out physical abnormalities before assuming that these somatic complaints are symptomatic of depression.

These symptoms are the key clinical manifestations of depression. The presence and severity of these symptoms can be established on the basis of interview information. A number of leading questions have been designed to evoke the patient's feelings that correspond to the components of the depressive syndrome. An outline of this procedure is provided in Lewinsohn and Lee (1981). It is important to keep in mind, however, that the only symptom present in almost all cases is dysphoria. The other five symptom clusters may or may not be evident, and each depressed individual may manifest different combinations of them. For this reason, depressed persons are not a single, or simple, target for treatment.

Magnitude of the Problem

Depression is a very common problem, and individuals for whom depression is either *the* or *a* problem constitute a large proportion of any clinician's case load. Conservative estimates indicate that at least four percent of the adult population is sufficiently depressed at any given time to warrant clinical treatment. At least twenty percent of the adult population will have a clinically significant episode of depression at some time in their lives (Amenson & Lewinsohn, 1981; Myers & Weissman, 1980). This means that over nine million Americans are currently clinically depressed, and more than forty million Americans will experience an episode of depression in their lifetimes. With these figures in mind, it is not surprising that depression has been called the common cold of mental health (e.g., Seligman, 1975). There is no doubt that depression is a serious problem—it exacts a heavy toll in

3

human suffering and is costly in terms of the demand that it places on mental health resources.

Epidemiological Considerations

One of the most consistent epidemiological findings concerning unipolar depression is a substantially higher rate of occurrence for females than for males. A ratio as high as 2:1 has frequently been reported in the literature (Weissman & Klerman, 1977). The prevalence of depression among women was further delineated in an extensive study of sex differences by Amenson and Lewinsohn (1981). It was found that for individuals without a history of depression, the percentages of women and men who became depressed during the study were very similar (7.1% vs. 6.9%). The results also indicated that women did not have longer episodes, nor were there any differences in age at first onset. The major difference between the sexes became apparent only when looking at the data for individuals with a previous history of depression. For this group, women were much more likely than men to become depressed again (21.8% vs. 12.9%). This suggests that women with a history of depression are at very high risk for subsequent episodes of depression.

The connection between age and depression is less well established. Gurland (1976) suggests that when psychiatric diagnosis is used as the criterion, high rates of depressive disorders are reported by individuals between 25 and 65 years of age, with a decrease in occurrence for younger and older groups. These data are probably distorted, however, by the tendency among the elderly not to use mental health services, and by the reluctance of clinicians to diagnose the elderly as depressed (Ernst, Badash, Beran, Kosovsky, & Kleinhauz, 1977). This problem in diagnosis may result in part from the confusion among clinicians and researchers in distinguishing between complaints due to the normal aging process and those that are due to a depressive disorder (Gurland, 1976; Raskin & Jarvik, 1979). It has been found that depression is frequently diagnosed as pseudo-dementia or senility by therapists working with the elderly.

The fact that depression is a time-limited and episodic phenomenon is another important epidemiological finding (e.g., Beck, 1967; Weissman & Paykel, 1974). For most individuals, episodes of depression are relatively short-lived but recurring (Lewinsohn, Fenn, & Franklin, 1982). Robins and Guze (1969) have reported a mean length for episodes of seven months; a median of 4.5 months was found by Amenson and Lewinsohn (1981).

Another clinically significant finding is that depressed individuals are at considerable risk for self-injurious and suicidal behavior. According to Lehman (1971), one out of every 200 depressed persons commits suicide. The

4

death rate from all causes for depressed females is twice the normal rate; for males it is triple the normal rate. Depressed women are more likely to attempt suicide; depressed men are more likely to succeed. It has been noted that the suicide rate for depressed patients is higher than for patients with any other psychological disorder (Becker, 1974; Mendels, 1975). These figures underscore the necessity for clinicians who are working with depressed clients to make a careful assessment of the risk of self-injurious and suicidal behavior. Clinicians should also be prepared to take appropriate preventive steps in those cases where the risk is judged to be high. It has been found that on the basis of relatively simple information, it is possible to make reasonably accurate predictions about the chance of serious suicidal behavior (e.g., Burglass & Horton, 1974). The issue of assessing suicide risk is discussed in more detail in Chapter 5.

The Need for a Cost-Effective Therapy

It is clear, both in terms of the magnitude of the problem and the cost and availability of mental health services, that most depressed individuals do not receive the kind of help that would be useful to them. In spite of efforts by organizations like the National Association for Mental Health and the National Institute of Mental Health, the general public still attaches negative connotations to being "mentally ill." As a result, many segments of the population (especially the elderly and low socioeconomic status people) are reluctant to seek psychiatric help until their problems are very severe. In addition, traditional psychotherapeutic services are expensive. The publicly supported services that are available often involve long waits and the quality of such services is variable. Although most episodes of depression are relatively short-lived, persons with a history of depression are at high risk for recurring episodes and for becoming "chronic" (Amenson & Lewinsohn, 1981). Therefore, treatment for depression must be designed to provide help quickly and to teach skills that allow persons who are prone to becoming depressed to prevent future episodes. In view of the above considerations, there is clearly a need for a nonstigmatizing, economical, easily accessible, and effective treatment for depression.

The Coping with Depression Course

A course entitled "Coping with Depression" is a new approach to the treatment of depression. The course is based on a social learning theory analysis which proposes that episodes of depression are associated with a decrease in pleasant and an increase in unpleasant person-environment interactions (see Chapter 2 for a more detailed discussion). No one is labeled "sick" or "crazy"; problems are not viewed as external manifestations of

5

physical imbalances or unconscious conflicts. Rather, problems are viewed as patterns of behavior and cognitions that have been learned and consequently can be unlearned or relearned within the context of the Coping with Depression course. The "therapist" is an instructor, the "treatment session" is a class, and the "patient/client" is a student. The course uses a format that is less stigmatizing and allows more outreach than traditional therapeutic strategies. It is a cost-effective treatment program that can be made available to a wide variety of depressed individuals.

The course employs lectures, class activities, homework assignments, a participant workbook, and a textbook to teach skills that have been shown to be particularly problematic for depressed individuals. The skills that are taught include time management, assertiveness, self-control techniques, self-monitoring, improving social skills, reducing anxiety, changing negative cognitions, and increasing pleasant and decreasing unpleasant activities. The course consists of twelve two-hour class sessions scheduled over eight weeks. Typically there are five to eight participants in each group. The course is highly structured and leads participants through a series of exercises designed to help them understand the relationship between their cognitions, the quality of their interactions, and their depressed mood.

Chapter 2

Theories Relating to the Coping with Depression Course

This chapter reviews the underlying theoretical and practical considerations that have played a major role in designing the components of the Coping with Depression course. The approach taken here has been heavily influenced by a social learning analysis of depression. This perspective emphasizes the importance of the quality and quantity of person-environment interactions as determinants for depression. The Coping with Depression course is somewhat eclectic, however, and has also incorporated components from cognitive therapies that have been shown to be effective in the treatment of depression. An overview of these approaches and their contribution to the Coping with Depression course is provided.

Social Learning Theory Analysis

According to social learning theory (Bandura, 1977), emotional disorders, previously considered to be external manifestations of internal (i.e., psychic) conflicts, are, in fact, behaviors that are influenced by the same laws of learning and development that influence normal behavior. "In the social-learning view, people are neither driven by inner forces nor buffeted by environmental stimuli. Rather, psychological functioning is explained in terms of continuous reciprocal interaction of personal and environmental determinants" (Bandura, 1977; p. 11). This interactionist view provides a

7

model of human behavior that considers normal and abnormal behavior as learned phenomena that influence (and are influenced by) person-environment interactions.

Contemporary social learning theory analysis assumes that depression is associated with a decrease in pleasant and an increase in unpleasant person-environment interactions (Lewinsohn, Youngren, & Grosscup, 1979). Depression and reinforcement are assumed to be related phenomena. The primary hypothesis states that a low rate of response-contingent positive reinforcement constitutes a critical antecedent for the occurrence of depression. Reinforcement is defined by the quality of the person's interactions with his or her environment. Those person-environment interactions with positive outcomes (i.e., outcomes making the person feel good) constitute a positive reinforcement arrangement. Person-environment interactions that are reinforced are strengthened. The term contingent refers to the connection between a particular behavior and its consequences; the reinforcement must follow the behavior. Social learning theory suggests that the behavior of depressed persons does not lead to positive reinforcement to a degree sufficient to maintain their behavior. Hence depressed persons find it difficult to initiate or to sustain their behavior and they become increasingly passive. A low rate of positive reinforcement is also assumed to cause the dysphoric mood that is central to the phenomenology of depression. The key notion is that depression results from too few person-environment interactions with positive outcomes.

A corollary hypothesis is that a high rate of punishing experience also causes depression. Punishment is defined as person-environment interactions with aversive (i.e., distressing, upsetting, unpleasant) outcomes. Punishing interactions with the environment may cause depression directly or indirectly by interfering with the person's engagement in, and enjoyment of, potentially rewarding activities.

There are three general reasons why a person may experience low rates of positive reinforcement and/or high rates of punishment: 1) the person's immediate environment may have few available positive reinforcers or may have many punishing aspects; 2) the person may lack the skills to obtain available positive reinforcers and/or to cope effectively with aversive events; 3) the positive impact of reinforcing events may be reduced and/or the negative impact of punishing events may be heightened.

These notions, and research results consistent with them, are discussed in more detail in Lewinsohn, Youngren, and Grosscup (1979). Their relevance for the treatment of depression is straightforward. To the extent that the theory is valid, treatment should increase the quantity and quality of the positively reinforcing person-environment interactions and decrease the quantity and quality of the punishing person-environment interactions. The depressed person is also assumed to have *learned* maladaptive reaction patterns that can be *unlearned* and replaced with more adaptive patterns. The model is described in layman's terms in Chapters 2 and 3 of *Control Your Depression.*

Recent Developments in the Psychological Treatment of Depression

During the past ten years there have been major conceptual and associated therapeutic developments in the outpatient treatment of depressed individuals. As recently as 1974, Becker observed that behaviorists have had relatively little to say about depression. Since then, at least 42 outcome studies of the behavioral treatment of depression have been reported and several major reviews have appeared (e.g., Hollon & Beck, 1978; Lewinsohn & Hoberman, 1982; Parloff, Wolfe, Hadley & Waskow, 1978; Rehm, 1981; Rehm & Kornblith, 1979).

Contemporary theoretical approaches may be roughly divided into those that emphasize "behavior" and those that emphasize "cognitions" in the etiology of depression. While these two conceptualizations differ in where they place the locus of causation, it is important to recognize their similarities. Both assume that the depressed patient has acquired maladaptive reaction patterns that can be unlearned. Symptoms are seen as important in their own right rather than as manifestations of underlying conflicts. The treatment approaches are focused upon the modification of relatively specific behaviors and cognitions rather than a general reorganization of the patient's personality.

Stimulated by these theoretical developments, there has been a proliferation of interventions and approaches for the psychological treatment of unipolar depression. Treatments derived from "cognitive" positions have been aimed at depressive thought processes (e.g., Beck, Rush, Shaw, & Emery, 1979; Fuchs & Rehm, 1977). In contrast, the treatments derived from "behavioral" approaches have been aimed at enhancing social skills (Sanchez, Lewinsohn, & Larson, 1980; Teri & Leitenberg, 1979; Zeiss, 1977), and improving pleasant activity level, time management, and relaxation skills (Grosscup & Lewinsohn, 1980) and at more general problem solving skills (McLean & Hakstian, 1979). In spite of this diversity, there is empirical support for the therapeutic efficacy of each approach (cf., Lewinsohn & Hoberman, 1982). The problem facing the practitioner at this point is one of *choosing* from among a range of promising conceptual formulations and therapeutic approaches.

A detailed analysis of each of the above mentioned treatments clearly shows that they employ overlapping behavioral and cognitive intervention strategies, including training in assertiveness, relaxation, self-control, decision making, problem solving, communication, time management, and increasing pleasant activities. Each strategy, either alone or in combination, has been shown to be effective in ameliorating depression. The Coping with Depression course was designed to incorporate the specific strategies shown to be effective, and thereby address those behaviors and cognitions that are problematic for depressed persons.

Common Components

The results of the above mentioned treatment outcome studies also pose an interesting theoretical problem. Since all of the treatments were theoretically derived, i.e., they were designed to modify the *specific* cognitions and/or behaviors assumed by the theory to be critical antecedents for depression, how could they *all* be effective? Furthermore, the treatments, while effective in ameliorating depression, do not seem to be specific in impacting the intervening target behaviors (and cognitions) at which they are aimed. Thus, in a recent study (Zeiss, Lewinsohn, & Muñoz, 1979) three treatments (cognitive, pleasant activities, and social skills training) were compared. The results indicated that while all three treatments were equally effective in reducing depression level, changes in the intervening dependent measures were not specific to the treatment. For example, the thinking of the patients in the social skills treatment changed as much as the thinking of those who were in the cognitive therapy treatment and vice versa; the pleasant activities of the patients in the pleasant activities treatment changed as much as the pleasant activities of those in the cognitive treatment, and so on.

On the basis of these results, Zeiss and colleagues (1979) advanced hypotheses as to what the critical components might be for a successful short-term cognitive-behavioral therapy for depression:

1. Therapy should begin with an elaborated, well-planned rationale. This rationale should provide the initial structure that guides the patient to the belief that he or she can control his or her own behavior, and thereby his or her depression.

2. Therapy should provide training in skills which the patient can utilize to feel more effective in handling his or her daily life. These skills must be of some significance to the patient and must fit with the rationale that has been presented.

3. Therapy should emphasize the independent use of these

skills by the patient outside of the therapy context and must provide enough structure so that the attainment of independent skill is possible for the patient.

4. Therapy should encourage the patient's attribution that improvement in mood is caused by the patient's increased skillfulness, not by the therapist's skillfulness (Zeiss, Lewinsohn, & Muñoz, 1979, pp. 437-438).

The Coping with Depression course was designed to incorporate these hypotheses.

Chapter 3

Selecting and Training Instructors

Over the last several years we have trained many instructors to lead the Coping with Depression course. Because instructor performance is critical to the success or failure of the course, we have made systematic evaluations of the factors relating to instructor effectiveness. Our experience suggests that instructors should be selected on the basis of their professional qualifications, personality characteristics, and level of clinical skills. During training it is essential for instructors to become thoroughly familiar with the components of the course, and to have the opportunity to lead one or more of the course sessions. Feedback from participants and supervision by experienced instructors are an important part of the training process. We have also found that instructor performance depends upon the implementation of effective teaching skills. This chapter has been included to help professionals in other settings select appropriate instructors and to offer guidelines for training them.

Selecting Instructors

The instructors for the Coping with Depression courses at the University of Oregon have been Ph.D. psychologists or advanced graduate students in Clinical and Counseling Psychology. Generally, the graduate students who have been trained to be instructors have completed several courses in psychopathology, assessment, and treatment. Although it is not necessary for instructors to have advanced professional degrees, it is essential for them to possess basic clinical skills. These skills should include the ability to reflect feelings, express warmth and empathy, shape and model appropriate non-depressive behaviors, summarize complex information, implement active listening skills, pinpoint problem areas, reframe problems so they are solvable, develop rapport, and establish a therapeutic alliance. In general, the graduate students that have been instructors for the Coping with Depression courses at the University of Oregon have had extensive clinical experience.

Thompson, Gallagher, Nies, and Epstein (1982) and Youngren (1978) have successfully trained paraprofessionals to conduct the course by providing them with highly specialized training and expert supervision. Thompson et al. (1982) suggest that the following considerations are important in the selection of course instructors:

1. Teaching the Coping with Depression course requires a substantial time commitment on the part of the instructors. Instructor-trainees who did not put in adequate time during training tended to have similar problems when they became instructors. They missed training sessions, were frequently late, and were often inadequately prepared.

2. A trainee's top priority should be learning to become an effective instructor. Those instructors whose motivation was based on improving their vitas or learning about "other" approaches to treatment tended to perform less well.

3. Because the course is based on a behavioral perspective, a potential instructor should be flexible enough to accept behavioral principles or at least test them. Those instructors who felt strongly that the behavioral approach was "too mechanistic" tended to deviate substantially from the designated treatment plan.

4. A potential instructor should be willing to tolerate and work with individuals experiencing psychological distress. Those individuals who became upset when they encountered distress in others were not able to function well as instructors.

5. A potential instructor should be well-organized. Planning sessions, presenting the material clearly, and keeping track of participants and their progress requires organization.

Instructor Training

Lewinsohn and his colleagues have used two different methods of training. One method (which was used in Antonuccio, Lewinsohn, & Steinmetz, 1982; Steinmetz, Lewinsohn, & Antonuccio, 1983; and Teri & Lewinsohn, 1982) requires student instructors to take the Coping with Depression course from a trained instructor. Potential instructors are expected to participate in all activities such as in-class exercises, homework, monitoring, tracking, and reading. In this way, potential instructors experience the participant's perspective and become familiar with the course structure and assignments. They also obtain a first-hand view of the types of problems encountered in leading the course and how skilled instructors handle them. We recommend that instructor-trainees have an opportunity to lead at least one of the sessions in order to become familiar with the instructor role and to get feedback from other participants regarding their performance. Another method of training instructors is to have novice instructors co-lead the course with an experienced instructor. This is the method that was used in Hoberman, Lewinsohn, and Tilson (in preparation).

Throughout training, course instructors should have opportunities for clinical supervision. This has typically consisted of regular weekly meetings with the other instructor-trainees and an experienced supervisor. Supervision should involve direct observation, case discussion, role playing, and modeling of techniques. It is important for course instructors to have ongoing interactions with one another; special problems always arise, and it is useful to share perspectives. Individual consultation with an experienced supervisor should also be available.

The Appropriate Role

Instructor Role vs. Therapist Role. Since most instructors of the Coping with Depression course will be trained psychotherapists, it may be useful to begin this discussion by contrasting the roles of "teacher" and "therapist." Regardless of theoretical orientation, the implicit and explicit role expectations are quite different. The Coping with Depression course leaders should always be conscious of the fact that in teaching the course they are instructors, not therapists.

A Therapist's Responsibilities. A therapist's primary responsibility is to the individual client. A therapist must be responsive to client complaints and must be willing to deal with unexpected crises and problems. Therapists must be willing to change their therapeutic approach in response to changes in the clinical conditions of the client (e.g., the client becomes more depressed, threatens suicide, or becomes psychotic). A therapist must also be willing to meet with the client at unscheduled times when the client faces an unexpected crisis.

An Instructor's Responsibilities. In contrast, an instructor's primary responsibility is to the class as a whole. An instructor's specific responsibilities to each individual participant are much more limited than the responsibilities of the therapist. This does not mean that the instructor is oblivious to individual problems, but it does mean that the instructor must continuously keep the needs of the group in mind. If a participant should experience a personal crisis while taking the course, the instructor is not expected to provide the necessary treatment. An instructor should serve as a source for information and referral and in this way provide for the needs of individual participants. To take an extreme example, if a participant is contemplating suicide, the instructor should refer that person to a therapist. The Coping with Depression course instructor has explicitly limited his or her role to that of an instructor whose major responsibility is teaching the participants the skills that are the components of the course. It is our belief that the instructor should not try to be a teacher and a therapist to the same person. Attempting this may cause the instructor to be ineffective in both roles.

Sometimes a participant will already be involved in therapy with another therapist. In this case, it is appropriate for the instructor and the therapist to communicate prior to the beginning of the course to insure congruent expectations between therapist, client, and course instructor. During the course, the client should be treated in the same manner as the other participants. Following termination of the course, and with the participant's permission, it is appropriate for the therapist and course instructor to again communicate, focusing on the participant's progress in the course.

Commonalities of the Therapist and Instructor Roles

There are, of course, many elements that the roles of instructor and therapist have in common. It is important that therapists and instructors give a convincing rationale for their respective approaches to treatment, and then use every opportunity to reinforce that rationale. In order to be effective, it is important for therapists and instructors to believe that the people with whom they work are capable of learning and changing their behavior. Therapists and instructors both strive to facilitate learning and create conditions conducive to behavior change.

An Illustrative Example. Imagine for a moment you are a participant in a small seminar on a topic in which you have a strong interest. Suppose that during class time one of the seminar members begins complaining at length about current marital difficulties. After a few minutes of listening, you may begin to feel that class time is being wasted because the class topic is not being addressed. The appropriate response on the part of the instructor would be to communicate to the student that unless the marital problems can somehow be related to the material being covered, the classroom is not the right setting to discuss this problem. In a similar fashion, the Coping with Depression course instructor should attempt to weave an individual participant's problems into the fabric of the course. This is not to say that the in-

16

structor should be insensitive, rejecting, or disinterested, but that the instructor's primary responsibility is to cover the class agenda. If dealing with a personal problem within the context of the course is not possible, then the instructor may want to set aside a period of time before or after class to discuss the participant's needs and offer appropriate assistance or referral.

The behavior of a group therapist in a similar situation, of course, would be entirely different. The group therapist would encourage the expression of individual problems and feelings within the context of the group process. The therapist would be willing to spend a considerable amount of time helping a participant work through his or her feelings concerning the marital situation and might call upon other group members to relate similar experiences.

Skills of Successful Instructors

The Coping with Depression instructor's primary goal is to effectively communicate and facilitate the acquisition of coping skills. Rosenshine and Furst (1971) reviewed several variables that seem to be related to effective teaching, most of which apply to leading the Coping with Depression course. The following is a discussion of some of the more important variables.

Clarity and Organization. The leader should present material in a clear and easily understood manner; material should be well organized. Chapter 6 provides a guide for effective course organization. In addition, it is strongly suggested that the leader use a blackboard to facilitate understanding concepts (e.g., by drawing diagrams or listing major points) and to delineate the organization of the material (e.g., by writing out the agenda before class). Use of other audiovisual aids is also encouraged.

Structuring Comments. Structuring comments that provide an overview of what is about to happen (or what has happened) help to clarify and organize the presented material. This aids the participants in processing the information. Again, writing the agenda on the blackboard before every session is a good way to clarify class structure.

Variability. The instructor should be flexible with regard to procedure and be willing to adapt to the needs of a particular group of participants. For example, if group members are uncomfortable about sharing personal information, breaking into small, task-oriented groups can often facilitate the interaction. Other breaks from a rigid format such as providing extra materials and displays can enhance learning the concepts.

Task Orientation. It is important for the instructor to keep the group focused on the task at hand. The instructor should take steps to redirect the discussion when it strays from the topic. In addition, the instructor can often encourage participants to help each other avoid depressive talk and focus on practical solutions based on the skills that they are learning. It should be pointed out that a task-oriented instructor is not necessarily insensitive—warmth and a genuine concern for participants are very important.

Enthusiasm. While instructor enthusiasm is a positive contribution to any course, it is particularly important in a course for depressed individuals. An instructor who understands the material well and is able to present it enthusiastically and confidently is more likely to motivate the participants to acquire new skills.

Use of Participants' Ideas. Using participants' ideas is an effective way to encourage participation and to personalize the concepts being taught. Flanders (1970) has suggested that the use of student ideas should include: 1) acknowledging the student's idea by repeating or paraphrasing the idea; 2) modifying the idea by rephrasing it or conceptualizing it in the teacher's own words; 3) applying the idea by using it to reach an inference or take the next step in a logical analysis of a problem; 4) comparing the idea with other ideas expressed earlier by the teacher or students; and 5) summarizing what has been said by an individual student or the entire class.

Avoidance of Criticism. There is a negative relationship between instructor criticism and the willingness of students to participate in class discussions. Even mild forms of criticism can have an adverse effect on the learning process. It is recommended that when leaders give feedback to participants, they should focus on the positive aspects of what the participant is doing and give positive rather than negative comments and suggestions.

Providing Opportunities to Learn. An important component of the teacher role is to provide each student with as many opportunities to learn the material as possible. During class, the instructor should make sure that the participants are on task and that each participant has a clear understanding of the material. It is important for the instructor to review the homework assignments carefully and give feedback to participants on how they are doing.

For participants, opportunity to learn means spending time on the material presented for each component of the course. If a participant does not attend a particular session, then an opportunity to learn has been lost. The instructor should contact participants soon after a meeting is missed in order to encourage their attendance at the next meeting and to help them problem-solve whatever difficulties they may be experiencing. An effective form of encouragement is to point out that their presence was missed and that each person makes a unique and integral contribution to the group.

Characteristics of Successful Instructors

Another set of studies that are potentially useful for describing successful Coping with Depression course instructors are the studies on the relationship between therapist characteristics and treatment outcome. This literature is succinctly reviewed by Parloff, Wolfe, Hadley, and Waskow (1978). Unfortunately, few clear generalizations have emerged and only a small number of therapist and process variables have been identified that correlate with treatment outcome. However, those variables that appear relevant to predicting which instructors are successful will be discussed briefly.

Instructor Emotional Problems. Although no outcome effects are clearly attributable to therapist personality characteristics, it seems reasonable to assume that instructors' problems may interfere with effective treatment. It is hypothesized that Coping with Depression course instructors who are less defensive, more relaxed, and happier are more effective in facilitating positive changes in their participants.

Instructor Experience. A few studies suggest that experienced therapists are more successful in achieving a favorable treatment outcome with their clients. It is recommended that Coping with Depression course instructors acquire experience before leading their first course.

Instructor Stylistic Variables. The studies of therapist stylistic characteristics are methodologically diverse and difficult to interpret. A study by Lieberman, Yalom, and Miles (1973) suggests that the most successful group therapists are those who provide a substantial amount of caring and interpreting, and moderate amounts of emotional stimulation and group direction.

Group Process Variables

Cohesiveness. The importance of group cohesion for positive therapeutic outcome has been reported in the literature (e.g., Yalom, 1975; Flowers & Booraem, 1980, 1981). In the Coping with Depression course, cohesiveness can be generated by encouraging participants to 1) give each other constructive and positive feedback whenever possible, 2) mingle socially during breaks and between classes, 3) help each other with their homework, and 4) work in small groups or on exercises designed to foster cooperative behavior.

Participation Level. Because the Coping with Depression course is structured like a class, a substantial proportion of the time is taken up with lecturing, instructor-participant interaction, and discussion moderated by the group instructor. Participant talking comprises approximately 30% of large group interaction. Additional interaction takes place during small group tasks. It is hypothesized that this approximates an optimal participation level. The instructor should be neither so dominant that the participants rarely interact with the instructor or among themselves, nor so submissive that the class gets out of control with nondirected discussion.

Chapter 4

Recruiting Participants

This chapter has been included to provide guidelines and suggestions for recruiting participants for Coping with Depression courses. The course is based on a group format designed for six to eight depressed participants; this insures that a group of reasonable size will remain even if one or two of the participants drop out. It is difficult to generate sufficient numbers of depressed individuals to offer the course through the conventional channels of self-referral or referral by professionals. We have found it necessary to make use of a broad assortment of methods to make the course widely known in the community and to encourage people to participate. The fact that many depressed individuals may feel too hopeless, too unmotivated, or do not think that they are depressed enough to seek help of their own accord, contributes to the need to actively advertise the availability of the course. Because we consider the course to be similar to other academic courses and self-help workshops, we feel that it is ethically acceptable to make use of a variety of community outreach procedures.

Making the Course Known in the Community
Utilization of Traditional Referral Sources
In making the course accessible to the community, it is important to use

the traditional means of seeking referrals. This can be accomplished by sending letters and announcements to mental health and social service agencies, psychiatrists, psychologists, social workers, counselors, and physicians (particularly general practitioners, internists, and pediatricians). These letters are designed to inform professionals about the nature and availability of the course (a sample letter is provided in Appendix 4.1). The course should be described as a psychoeducational approach that teaches individuals skills to overcome their depression. Professionals may be more receptive to the course if it is portrayed as an inexpensive treatment that may be considered an adjunctive service that need not replace ongoing therapy. We have found that these letters are more effective if they are supplemented by individual contacts, lectures, and articles in the newsletters of professional organizations.

Utilization of Nontraditional Sources

Television and radio. Although we know of no such data, it is probably safe to assume that many depressed people spend a great deal of time watching television or listening to the radio. Consequently, television and radio have been used to reach potential participants. Public service announcements and local talk shows are an excellent means for obtaining free media coverage. Talk shows not only publicize the course but also provide the public with information on depression and the types of treatments that are available. These services can be obtained by letting the media know about the availability of the course via a "news release." A sample radio and television news release is provided in Appendix 4.2. Paid advertising is more costly but also allows for more control in that you choose the station, the content, and when announcements are made.

Newspaper. Our most dependable source of potential participants has been newspaper advertising (see Appendix 4.3 for a sample display ad). Our experience has been that newspaper display advertisements, although relatively expensive, generate a steady flow of calls. A less expensive (and less reliable) medium is classified advertising. Feature stories in the local newspaper, like television and radio talk shows, serve the dual function of publicizing the course and providing information to the public about the treatment of depression.

Public circulars. We have found it useful to post and distribute announcements in public places (such as schools, supermarkets, senior centers, and laundromats) and in local businesses and agencies. In addition, information about the course should be sent to the staff of newsletters published by community colleges, industrial organizations, neighborhood newspapers, and specialty newsletters (see Appendix 4.4).

Letters to previous students. In the long run, recommendations from former participants are probably the most reliable source of new participants. For this reason, it is worthwhile to send occasional announcements to former participants advising them that the courses are still being offered and asking them to recommend the course to depressed friends and/or family members (see Appendix 4.5).

Ethical Considerations

The ethical concerns of publicizing the Coping with Depression course to depressed patients must be seriously considered, especially when nontraditional advertising procedures are involved. It is important that potential instructors be familiar with the ethical guidelines of their profession. Before advertising, psychologists should be aware of the "Ethical Principles of Psychologists" and "Standards for Providers of Psychological Services" published by the American Psychological Association (1981). Especially relevant are the ethical principles which are reproduced in Appendix 4.6 pertaining to Public Statements.

As an instructor it is important for you to be aware that you are responsible for your actions and the consequences that follow. Public statements should always be accurate and objectively specify your qualifications and what can be expected from your approach. A clear description of the course and its purpose should also be provided. The information should aid the potential consumer in making appropriate judgments and choices. In any written or spoken publicity campaign concerning the course, it is important to treat all claims of performance with professional integrity and to be careful not to offer promises regarding outcome. Participants should be given a realistic appraisal of what they might accomplish; promoting false hopes can be potentially debilitating to depressed individuals.

The APA Ethical Guidelines are quite clear about what can and cannot be done in advertising (APA, 1981). Public statements should *not* contain: 1) a false, fraudulant, misleading, deceptive, or unfair statement; 2) a misinterpretation of fact or a statement likely to mislead or deceive; 3) a testimonial from a patient; 4) a statement intended to (or likely to) create false or unjustified expectations of favorable results.

Planning a Media Campaign

Since a certain amount of time is necessary for the information to reach its intended audience and for that audience to initiate contact, we have typically begun our media campaign at least two months before the beginning of a course. We have found that an ongoing evaluation of media campaigns facilitates the planning of future campaigns and makes it possible to regu-

23

late the response rate during any given campaign. One easy method we have employed is to ask those inquiring about the course how they heard about it. We then keep track of their responses as well as what campaign strategy we were employing at the time of the call.

The size of the recruitment campaign will vary as a function of the number of students needed for the course. We have found, however, that *some* type of media campaign is critical for producing the number of participants necessary to start even one group. It is only after the course is fairly well known in the community that one can count on a steady trickle of referrals and depressed individuals seeking to participate in the course. Any recruitment campaign, no matter how brief, represents an expenditure of time and money and has a potential impact on you, your clients, your community, and your profession. With careful planning, the campaign can be quite successful.

Initial Contacts with Potential Participants

Mental health professionals who are interested in offering the Coping with Depression course should find the procedures already described in this chapter to be effective in generating potential participants. The next step in recruiting participants is to provide them with detailed information about the nature of the course and what will be expected of them. This makes it possible for potential participants to make an informed decision as to whether or not the approach offered in the course is right for them. Professional ethics dictate that it is very important to keep the welfare of the individual in mind—potential participants *must* understand what is going to take place during the course before they are enrolled. Typically, this is accomplished during the initial phone call and interview described below.

Handling Telephone Responses

When potential participants call to inquire about the course, they should be given enough information to decide whether or not they would like to come in for an interview. It is our experience that this first contact is critical and must be handled by a well-trained person who is thoroughly familiar with all aspects of the course. We have found it very useful to provide the receptionist with a "script" that describes the course in detail, suggests responses to questions that are likely to be asked, and indicates the procedures that should be followed if the person is interested in enrolling in the course (see Appendix 4.7).

It is also our experience that approximately one-half of the people who call and inquire about the course actually enroll. Therefore, professionals or agencies who are offering the course should be prepared to set aside an adequate amount of time to handle incoming phone calls. If a successful recruitment campaign generates more participants than can be accomodated, alternate resources should be made available.

The Interview

When potential participants come in for an interview, they are given specific information about the nature of the course, what is (and what is not) discussed in class sessions, the types of responsibilities expected of participants and instructors, and so on. It is not until the end of the interview that participants decide whether or not to enroll in the course. During the interview they are encouraged to ask any questions they may have regarding aspects of the course that they do not fully understand. The interviewer should be prepared to answer all questions that arise and should be willing to spend enough time to be thorough. This approach is critical because it insures that potential participants are completely informed before they make their decision to enroll in the course. A second purpose of this interview is to assess the appropriateness of the individual as a participant in the course. To accomplish this, the interviewer will need to complete the intake procedures that are outlined in Chapter 5 of this book. It should be noted that the interview process requires a considerable amount of staff time. However, it is a very important part of setting up the Coping with Depression course, and efforts should not be made to reduce the time spent conducting interviews. Once the individual decides to enroll in the course, he or she should sign a statement of informed consent such as the one provided in Appendix 4.8.

Chapter 5

Intake Procedures/
Selecting
Participants

The purpose of this chapter is to outline the intake procedures that should be followed before enrolling a potential participant in the Coping with Depression course. These procedures are used not only as a basis for excluding individuals who are not appropriate for this treatment, but also to provide extensive background information on participants. The background material obtained on an individual during intake assessment is extremely useful for pinpointing deficits in specific coping skills that may be contributing to occurrences of depression.

Intake Assessment

Depression

Because the course is specifically designed to alleviate depression, the first step during intake is to establish the presence and severity of the disorder. This task is made particularly difficult by the fact that depressed individuals are a relatively diverse group exhibiting a broad range of symptoms. As a result, the assessment of depression should be carried out using several different diagnostic systems and interview techniques. The following is a survey of the assessment procedures that are suggested for intake purposes.

The most intensive and detailed method for arriving at a diagnosis of depression is to use a structured clinical interview in conjunction with a reliable diagnostic system. The Schedule for Affective Disorders and Schizophrenia—Lifetime version (SADS-L; Endicott & Spitzer, 1978) is a two-hour, structured interview that systematically assesses a wide variety of symptoms. It covers a range of psychiatric disorders with primary emphasis on unipolar depressive, bipolar, schizophrenic, and schizo-affective disorders. The SADS-L focuses on differential diagnosis and is designed to systematically rule in, or rule out, specific diagnoses by using a decision-tree format. The source for obtaining the SADS-L is provided in Appendix 5.1. The *Diagnostic and Statistical Manual of Mental Disorders—III* (DSM-III; American Psychiatric Association, 1980) and the Research Diagnostic Criteria (RDC; Spitzer, Endicott, & Robins, 1978) are elaborate classification systems which have been designed for clinical and research purposes, respectively. The DSM-III distinguishes among three subtypes of unipolar depression (major, dysthymic, and atypical) and three subtypes of bipolar depression (bipolar, cyclothymic, and atypical bipolar). The DSM-III criteria are listed in Appendix 5.2. The highly reliable RDC describes ten non-mutually exclusive subtypes of depression; to date, however, these subtypes have not been shown to have implications for treatment. The source for obtaining the RDC is provided in Appendix 5.3. Although clinicians are not likely to use the complete SADS-L or RDC for routine assessment purposes, the clinician should become familiar with these instruments to identify probes that are useful for evaluating depressed individuals. The SADS-Change version (SADS-C; Endicott & Spitzer, 1978) is a shorter adaptation of the SADS-L that can be used to streamline pre- and post-treatment assessments. When used together, the SADS-L (or SADS-C) and RDC are a fairly reliable, cost-effective, diagnostic evaluation system.

A less time consuming method of assessing the presence and severity of depression involves ratings of specific symptoms or symptom clusters by the clinician. Several well-known scales are available including the Feelings and Concerns Checklist (Grinker et al., 1961) and the Hamilton Rating Scale for Depression (Hamilton, 1960). Both of these scales reliably discriminate depressed from nondepressed individuals. Within depressed populations they also differentiate clients with varying degrees of symptom severity. Because depressed persons manifest symptoms in different combinations and with different intensities, each client will have a unique pattern of scores. Rating scales typically cover six general categories of symptoms: dysphoria, reduced rate of behavior, social-interactional problems, guilt, feelings of material burden, and somatic complaints. A short version of the Feelings and Concerns Checklist is provided in Appendix 5.4.

Self-report measures take only a few minutes to administer and can be used to substantiate interviewer impressions. These brief questionnaires are an efficient method for screening individuals before conducting a more extensive diagnostic interview. The Beck Depression Inventory (BDI; Beck et al., 1961) consists of 21 items. The BDI has frequently been used as a pre- and post-treatment measure for participants in the Coping with Depression course. The time frame sampled by the BDI is "the way you feel today." The expected BDI is the same questionnaire but the instructions ask individuals to describe the way they expect to feel at the *end* of the course; it is interesting to note that the expected BDI has been shown to be relatively accurate in predicting treatment outcome. The BDI and expected BDI are provided in Appendices 5.5 and 5.6 respectively. The Center for Epidemiologic Studies—Depression scale (CES-D; Radloff, 1977) is a 20-item self-report scale. The CES-D is a highly reliable and valid self-report depression inventory that samples feelings of depression for the previous week. The CES-D was developed to measure symptoms of depression in the general population, and extensive normative data are available (Radloff, 1977). The CES-D is provided in Appendix 5.7.

Individuals meeting the following criteria are considered to be clinically depressed: 1) a BDI score ≥ 11; 2) a CES-D score ≥ 8; or 3) mean symptom ratings on all Feeling and Concerns Checklist factors $\geq .70$ and a dysphoria factor score ≥ 1.0. It should be noted, however, that an individual does not necessarily need to be clinically depressed in order to participate in the Coping with Depression course. If someone feels depressed and wants to participate in the course, he or she should be given an opportunity to do so.

Suicidal Behavior

The evaluation of a depressed individual should also include an assessment of suicidal behavior. It has been shown that the suicide rate among depressives is higher than among patients with any other diagnosis (Miles, 1977). The task for the clinician is to evaluate the risk of suicide for each client. Several risk factors have been shown to be possible antecedents for suicidal behavior. The Suicidal Risk Rating Form developed by Lettieri (1974) has grouped these factors according to sex and age, and given a weight to each item. When totalled, these weights give a range and rating for risk of suicide from low to high. Another assessment tool using risk factors is the SAD PERSONS scale (Patterson, Dohn, Bird, and Patterson, 1983). SAD PERSONS is an acronym for ten major risk factors: sex, age (less than 19, greater than 45), depression, previous attempt, ethanol abuse, rational thinking loss, social support, organized plan, no spouse, and sickness (i.e., physical illness). One point is given for each factor; persons with a total that is between 7 and 10 should be considered at serious risk for a suicide attempt. This scale is straightforward, easy to use, and has been shown to be both reliable and valid in the evaluation of suicidal behavior. Since previous suicide attempts are highly predictive of suicidal behavior (Patterson et al., 1983), a Suicide Attempt Interview is included in the intake procedures for the Coping with Depression program (see Appendix 5.8). This interview includes information on past suicidal ideation, number of previous attempts, and the circumstances, means, and consequences of each attempt.

Social Support

Recently, both researchers and clinicians have shown increasing interest in the connection between social support and feelings of well-being. Social support systems seem to act indirectly, serving as a buffer against the consequences of stress. Intimacy (defined as a close, confiding relationship with a spouse or confidant) seems to act as a moderating variable between stressful life events and the onset of depression. Women have been found to be less likely to develop depression if they have a confiding relationship (Brown & Harris, 1978). Social support may also directly influence feelings of well-being, independent of stress, by serving as an agent for behavior change.

The Brown Intimacy scale (Appendix 5.9) uses a four-point system to evaluate social support: "A" means that the client has an intimate and confiding relationship with a spouse, "B" and "C" indicate a relationship with other confidants, and "D" is used if the client has no close relationships. In addition to the Intimacy Scale, it is useful to assess *changes* in the social support system (e.g., an increase or decrease in the number and quality of relationships). Such changes may be a particular problem for the client because they tend to increase the likelihood and severity of depressive episodes.

The Social Adjustment Scale (Weissman and Paykel, 1974) assesses the patterns of interpersonal relationships in detail (Appendix 5.10). The SAS is a semistructured interview consisting of questions about five areas: work, social leisure, extended family, marital, and parental. Each question is given a rating of 1 to 5, and a global score is established for each of the areas.

Medical and Physical Condition

The Medical Condition Interview (Appendix 5.11) should be used to make an assessment of the participant's physical health. In some cases an existing medical disorder, or medication prescribed for a medical disorder, may be responsible for episodes of depression. The connection between depressive symptoms and a variety of physical conditions (e.g., chronic disease or disabling handicap) and pharmacological agents has been well estab-

30

lished (Hall, Popkin, Devaul, Faillace, & Stickney, 1978). It is particularly important in working with elderly individuals to obtain a comprehensive medical history, including records of a current physical examination, to rule out depression that is secondary to a medical condition or to medications.

Reading Level

Because the course is structured as a class that requires reading assignments from a text and homework from a student workbook, it is important to discourage potential participants with reading difficulties and/or learning disabilities from taking the course. For this reason, it is recommended that intake procedures include administering the Level II reading subtest of the Wide Range Achievement Test or WRAT (Jastak and Jastak, 1978). The source for obtaining the WRAT is listed in Appendix 5.12.

Selecting Participants and Final Intake Procedures

Exclusion Criteria

Consistent with the educational philosophy of the course, exclusion criteria have been kept to a minimum. More than 90 percent of the individuals who decide that they would like to participate in the course after coming in for the initial interview are accepted for enrollment. The main consideration is whether the individual is going to be able to function well within the treatment format (i.e., complete the readings and assignments and work with others as a member of a structured group) and benefit from the course. To this end, persons with dyslexia, acute psychotic features, serious organic impairments, severe alcohol or drug addiction problems, or serious hearing or sight impairments, have been consistently excluded from taking the course; a referral for other treatment has usually been provided. Individuals showing evidence of bipolar depression or acute suicidal tendencies should be referred for concurrent treatment (e.g., psychotropic drug therapy or one-to-one psychotherapy, respectively); they may participate in the course, however, if they receive additional treatment. Concurrent psychological or psychiatric treatment and/or psychotropic medication have not been considered to be exclusion criteria. People with acute marital conflict may enroll in the Coping with Depression course with the goal of reducing depression. Although marital relationships may benefit indirectly from the course, it should not be the primary motivation for enrolling. A referral for additional therapy may be necessary for those who are experiencing extreme marital discord.

Background Information

After the intake interview has been completed, it is recommended that the interviewer summarize background information in a brief write-up (a form is provided in Appendix 5.13). Because the assessment devices just reviewed generate a considerable amount of detail, a summary of key points is particularly important. This can be done informally with the interviewer making some notes on impressions of the participant's problem areas and possible intervention strategies to bring about changes in these areas. A description of the participant's interview behavior (e.g., affect, physical appearance, and psychomotor functioning) may also be useful when contrasted with improvements achieved during the course. After the course begins, it is suggested that the instructor keep weekly notes on the progress of each participant and that these notes be kept in the assessment file. It should also be noted that a more structured format for the write-up is included with the SADS.

Instructor/Participant Meeting

After prospective participants have been interviewed and determined to be appropriate candidates for the course, and after they have made a commitment to participate, the final step in the intake process is an individual meeting between each participant and the instructor. This meeting allows them to become acquainted, and gives the instructor an opportunity to present an overview and rationale for the course. The instructor should make sure that the participant has accurate expectations about the course and should emphasize that successful acquisition and subsequent incorporation of these skills into everyday life will depend upon the participant's own efforts. During this meeting the participant is given *Control Your Depression* and the *Participant Workbook,* as well as the first homework assignment which consists of completing the Pleasant Events Schedule and certain readings.

Chapter 6

Course Description

This chapter describes in detail the twelve sessions that constitute the Coping with Depression course. It is an expanded version of the instructor's manual that was written in 1979 by Steinmetz, Antonuccio, Bond, McKay, Brown, and Lewinsohn. The material presented here is intended to serve as a semistructured guide for course instructors. Although a detailed agenda and outline have been included for each session, it is essential for instructors to be familiar with the literature and concepts relating to the topic areas that are covered by the course sessions. Recommended readings are listed for several of the sessions to provide instructors with a resource for obtaining additional background information. Because the Coping with Depression Course is offered in a group format, issues concerning group dynamics are particularly important. The book by Yalom (1975) may be very useful for instructors who do not have a working knowledge of group process variables.

The Coping with Depression Course consists of twelve two-hour sessions conducted over eight weeks. Sessions are held twice a week (three days apart) during the first four weeks of treatment, and once a week for the final four weeks. Follow-up sessions called "class reunions" are held one month and six months after treatment to facilitate the maintenance of treatment gains. The first two sessions of the course are devoted to defining the ground rules, presenting the social learning view of depression, and teaching basic self-change skills. The next eight sessions are devoted to acquiring skills in four specific areas: learning how to relax, increasing pleasant activities, changing negative cognitions, and improving social skills/increasing positive social interaction. Two sessions are dedicated to each skill. The final two sessions focus on maintenance and prevention issues; each participant is encouraged to develop a personalized plan to continue to work on specific problem areas on a regular basis by using the skills and techniques learned in the course. The class reunions provide a sense of continuity for the participants, and help them to stay motivated to periodically monitor their depression level and make use of their new coping skills.

Although the course is customarily conducted in a small-group format (six to eight participants per course) it may also be offered on a one-to-one basis (individual tutoring) or in a self-help modality with periodic telephone consultation with the course instructor. Brown and Lewinsohn (1984b) evaluated the relative efficacy of the course in these three modalities and found them to be equally effective in reducing depression. The group modality may be preferable, as it is the most efficient use of the instructor's time and allows for social interaction and group problem-solving among the participants. Classes also seem to be more stimulating and challenging in that a variety of problems and successes is available for group discussion. In addition, although we have no data to support it, leader "burn out" seems to be a less serious problem for group instructors than for instructors engaged in individual tutoring.

Consistent with an educational format, the Coping with Depression course makes use of the textbook *Control Your Depression* by Lewinsohn, Muñoz, Youngren and Zeiss (1986) and a *Participant Workbook* by Brown and Lewinsohn (1984a). The workbook includes a course syllabus, previews of each session, detailed homework assignments, and forms for skill acquisition and progress monitoring. These forms are larger and more functional versions of the forms that appear in *Control Your Depression*.

Each session follows a similar format. The instructor develops an agenda and writes it on the blackboard at the beginning of each class. A typical agenda consists of announcements, a review of material and homework from the previous session, a lecture on new material, discussion and exercises related to the new material, a preview of the next unit, and a homework assignment. Homework assignments are designed so that participants begin collecting baseline data relevant to the skill presented in the next session before they hear the lecture on that material. Each agenda also includes a "pep talk" and a break. The pep talk was instituted because we have found that at each stage of the course certain comments and observations help to keep group morale high and encourage open communication about the group's progress. Although suggested pep talks are included in the outline for each session, instructors should feel free to use this time to address salient group-process issues. A break is provided approximately halfway through each session. About 15 minutes should be set aside for informal chatting, visits to the restroom, and refreshment. We customarily supply coffee and tea, and participants often contribute cookies or other snacks. The break provides an opportunity for informal socialization among group members and also gives participants a chance to speak with the instructor privately or obtain remedial consultation. It is important for instructors to make themselves available to participants during breaks.

There are several conventions that have been used in this part of the book to make it easier for instructors to use it as a lecture outline. Most of the material is meant to be shared with the class participants and is written so that it may be read out loud. Consequently, the perspective is second person (e.g., "The assignment is for you to monitor your daily mood. . . .") Other parts are intended for the instructor only and are not to be presented as part of the lecture to the class. This material has been printed in italics.

Session 1
Depression and
Social Learning

The first session will be described in considerable detail. It is a particularly important session because an overview of the course is provided and ground rules (group norms) are established. In traditional therapy groups, process issues are allowed to evolve and are then used for therapeutic interaction. The social psychology of small group dynamics also supports the idea that newly formed groups need to spend some time to clarify and, if possible, achieve consensus on group norms. However, rather than waiting for problems to evolve and then be solved, we have found that it is a better strategy to anticipate the problems that are most likely to occur and establish group rules to circumvent them. The time-limited and educational format of the Coping with Depression course makes it necessary for the instructor to take a strong role in delineating the ground rules at the beginning of the course.

The social learning approach to depression is also presented during the first session. Because these concepts are the theoretical underpinnings of the Coping with Depression course, it is recommended that instructors take the time to provide an in-depth explanation of social learning principles. It is our impression that the effectiveness of the course is determined at least in part by the degree to which participants "buy into" the underlying rationale for the course. Although some examples are given in the lecture outline for the session, it may be useful to offer additional examples to illustrate important concepts.

AGENDA

   I. BUSINESS
  II. PEP TALK
 III. INTRODUCTION AND GROUND RULES
 IV. GET ACQUAINTED EXERCISE
  V. THE SOCIAL LEARNING APPROACH
 VI. REVIEW SESSION 1 HOMEWORK
VII. PREVIEW SESSION 2 AND ASSIGN HOMEWORK

*   *   *

I.   BUSINESS

   A. Introduce class members to each other as they arrive for the first time.

   B. Make sure everyone has Control Your Depression *and the* Participant Workbook for the Coping with Depression Course.

   C. Draw a small seating chart to help remember names.

II.   PEP TALK (suggested)

   A. **It is always difficult to get started on something new.** Congratulations, you have taken the first step by enrolling in this course and coming to the first session. At this point it may be helpful to imagine that you are a sprinter in a race; as you look down the track you know that winning the race will depend upon getting off to a good start. It is equally important to get a good start in this course by doing a thorough job on the first assignment.

   B. **This course has a lot to offer you, but it will only be effective if you actively try to make changes in your life.** The benefits that you receive from this course are largely determined by your willingness to keep an open mind and try new things.

C. **You can learn to control your depression and improve your mood.** Most people entering this course feel that they have little or no control over their mood. In this course you will learn to identify some of the events that influence your behavior and the way that you feel. Particular attention will be given to helping you develop skills to regulate your mood and prevent depression.

III. INTRODUCTION AND GROUND RULES

A. Introduction.

1. **Depression is the result of "problems in living."** The social learning perspective suggests that occurrences of unipolar depression can be explained by looking at the balance between positive and negative outcomes from interactions with the environment. This is in contrast to medical models that regard depression as a disease and stress the importance of biochemical processes as determinants of depression. The underlying idea of the social learning approach is very straightforward—interactions with positive outcomes make you feel good, while interactions with negative outcomes make you feel bad. When the balance between positive and negative outcomes becomes increasingly negative, your mood and sense of well-being are adversely affected. The Coping with Depression course is an opportunity to systematically work on your interactions with the environment so that more positive outcomes occur.

2. **The Coping with Depression course is skill and task oriented, not an encounter group.** Although it is understood that you may have many important issues to talk about, the purpose of the class is to focus on learning new skills. You can expect to be very busy with the work involved in learning how to gain control over your mood, so it is important that you stay on task. Group discussion is expected to be constructive and specific rather than abstract and theoretical. The group dynamics of the Coping with Depression course may be quite different from other group therapy experiences that you may have had.

3. **Homework assignments are required.** Perhaps the most important part of the course occurs between sessions as you carry out your homework assignments and practice the skills that you have learned in class. It is important to remember that doing the homework will help you to gain more from the course. If you are experiencing problems with your homework, it is appropriate to contact me either before or after the class and ask for assistance.

4. **Students are responsible for learning new skills.** The material for this course will be presented in a systematic and understandable manner. Ultimately, however, the responsibility for learning falls upon you as a participant in this course.

5. **The instructor is a teacher and facilitator.** The role of the instructor is not to provide therapy for individual students but to present the material to the group and to help maximize the opportunities for learning.

6. **This course is an opportunity for you to learn new and useful skills to control your mood.** These skills include learning how to relax, increasing pleasant activities, changing aspects of one's thinking, improving social skills, and increasing positive social interactions.

7. **At the end of the course, the skills that work for you will be used to develop a life plan.** It is hoped that by becoming familiar with several coping skills you will learn which ones work best for you and that you will integrate these skills into your life. Developing a life plan will help you to maintain the benefits that you derive from this course.

8. **The course is not therapy or counseling.** If at any time during the course you should feel a need to see a therapist, I will be more than willing to provide an appropriate referral.

B. **Ground Rules.**

We have found that it is necessary for instructors to spend a considerable amount of time making sure that the participants follow the ground rules as closely as possible.

Certain ground rules have been established for the course and it is important for these rules to be spelled out as early as possible. These ground rules are designed to facilitate the learning process and allow everyone an equal chance to take part in class activities and discussions.

1. **Avoid depressive talk.** Use the group for support, not as a sounding board for your depression. It is important to help each other get away from depressive talk.

2. **Be supportive.** Avoid criticizing others; try to keep feedback constructive. Caring for others means being supportive and thoughtful. Try to reward others by finding the positive aspects of what they are saying. It is important to remain noncoercive—irritable and angry reactions to others are not appropriate and tend to be destructive to group interactions.

3. **Provide equal time.** In order for all class members to benefit as much as possible from the course, everyone should have an opportunity to share ideas, ask questions, and discuss difficulties that they may encounter in applying the techniques. Adherence to the "equal time" ground rule is often difficult. However, it is important that this ground rule be followed to insure that everyone has an equal opportunity to learn.

The instructor should try to draw out shy participants and to cut off participants who tend to dominate class discussions. Encourage shy class members to participate by addressing questions to them; when they respond, make a special effort to build upon their ideas and relate some common experiences. Cutting off a dominating class member may prove to be a little more difficult. However, by listening carefully to what the person is saying, it is usually possible to paraphrase and draw comparisons to material that the group has discussed and, in this way, shift the attention to another person or agenda item. These issues are discussed in detail in Chapter 7.

4. **Confidentiality.** It is important to honor the confidentiality of personal information that is offered in group sessions. You are expected not to discuss information relating to the personal matters of other participants with anyone—the privacy of others must be respected. Any information discussed in the intake interview will remain confidential and will not be shared with the group.

IV. GET ACQUAINTED EXERCISE

Organize groups consisting of two or three participants and have them share information about their backgrounds and areas of interest.

You might suggest that participants try to describe themselves in a positive light. Then, regroup and have participants introduce one another to the rest of the class.

The first exercise is to get to know each other. The class will be divided into smaller groups so that you will feel more comfortable sharing information about your background and areas of interest. By the end of the exercise you should know the names of the persons in your group and something specific about them.

BREAK

V. RATIONALE AND OVERVIEW OF THE SOCIAL LEARNING APPROACH TO DEPRESSION

A. Ways of thinking about depression.

1. Depression is a disease.

   a. This approach assumes that depression is due to some underlying pathology.

   b. It is necessary to go to a medical doctor or a specialist for treatment.

   c. Bipolar depression is the only type of depression that is known to be a medical problem, however; the best treatment available is lithium.

2. Depression is related to problems in living (our view).

   a. This approach suggests that people need a favorable balance between interactions with positive outcomes and those with negative or neutral outcomes.

   b. Depression is a signal that there is something lacking or off balance.

   c. There are multiple roads to depression.

      1) Interactions that were a source of positive outcomes are no longer available (e.g., someone close to you dies or moves away).

41

2) The necessary skills for eliciting positive outcomes from interactions are lacking.

3) Skills are needed to change the quantity and quality of interactions.

4) This course is designed to teach some of those skills.

5) We will try to provide a convincing rationale for each technique.

3. Behavior, thinking, and emotions: a three-faceted mutually interactive system.

   a. Behavior. In simple terms, behavior is how we interact with our environment (for example, how we interact with others).

      1) Depressive behaviors are those behaviors associated with unpleasant or dissatisfying outcomes, (i.e., behaviors that have negative consequences.)

      2) Nondepressive behaviors are those behaviors associated with positive outcomes, (e.g., behaviors that give us feelings of competence and personal fulfillment.)

   b. Thinking. The quality of our thoughts regarding our interactions with our environment is a very important factor.

      1) Depressive thinking involves thoughts that are negative or self-deprecating (thoughts that one is useless, boring, unattractive, stupid, incompetent, and so on).

      2) Nondepressive thinking is characterized by positive self-statements and self-enhancing statements.

   c. Emotions. Feelings give us a global index of how our life is going. The tendency is to try to make changes in this area first, but it is the most difficult area in which to intervene. We will focus on the other two areas with the understanding that by changing behaviors and thoughts, emotions also change.

B. The premise of the course is that people who are depressed have learned to behave, think, and feel depressed.

C. The depressive cycle may start anywhere in this triad:

1. Feelings and emotions, behavior, and thinking.

Feelings and Emotions

Behavior   **Thinking**

Illustration: When we feel bad we are less likely to initiate behaviors and we have doubts about our ability to engage successfully in the behavior. When we are successful at something we feel good and we gain self-confidence. When we feel that we can do something well we are more likely to initiate the action.

2. This can be visualized as a feedback loop.

   a. How you feel affects how you think and behave, which affects how you feel, and so on.

   b. This is a mutually interactive system—each facet affects the others.

3. The depressive spiral.

   a. Few positive outcomes.

   b. Feel depressed.

   c. Do less.

   d. Thoughts become increasingly negative.

   e. Feel even worse, then do less, etc.

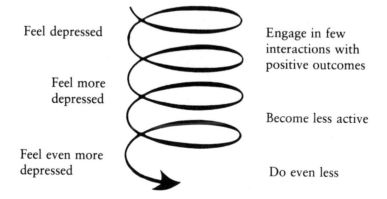

Feel depressed   Engage in few
                                        interactions with
                                        positive outcomes

     Feel more
     depressed   Become less active

Feel even more
depressed   Do even less

D. A positive spiral is also possible.

   1. The strategy is to intervene in the negative cycle and change it.

   2. The tendency is to try to intervene in the emotional facet, that is, to try to feel better first; but this is the hardest to change.

   3. It is less difficult to intervene at the thinking and behavior levels—this leads to changes in feelings and emotions.

E. This course is a survey of skills that can change this depressive spiral.

   1. The skill areas related to the behavior facet are:

      a. Pleasant activities.

      b. Social skills.

   2. The skill areas related to the thinking facet are:

      a. Constructive thinking.

      b. Balancing positive and negative thoughts.

   3. The skill area related to the feeling facet is relaxation.

VI. **REVIEW SESSION 1 HOMEWORK**

   A. Are there any questions about the reading assignment? The assignment for this session was handed out at the interview prior to beginning the course.

      1. Complete the Pleasant Events Schedule.

      2. Read Chapters 1, 2, and 3 in *Control Your Depression (CYD)* after completing the Pleasant Events Schedule.

      3. Begin monitoring daily mood (see pp. 38-40 in *CYD*).

   B. Mood monitoring.

      1. Problems remembering? Try doing it at the same time each night.

      2. Remember to record your average mood for the day.

      3. Anchor mood ratings by writing down specific situations or feelings that go along with ratings of "the most depressed I have ever felt" through "the happiest I have ever felt."

VII. PREVIEW SESSION 2 AND ASSIGN HOMEWORK

A. Preview: Self-change.

1. In the next session we will cover basic skills that are the foundation for the rest of the course.

2. Self-change is different from will power. Self-change is a skill that you can learn.

3. There are three critical ingredients for self-change.

   a. The belief that you can change.

   b. Recognizing that self-change is a skill you can learn.

   c. Developing an action plan.

B. *Assign homework. Have students turn to Session 2 in the* Participant Workbook. *Go over the goals of the session and the homework assignment; make sure that you explain the relevant tracking forms.*

1. Continue mood rating.

2. Read Chapter 4 in *CYD.*

3. Fill out figure 4-1 on page 57. Read pages 55, 56, and 58 carefully, and assign priorities to your problems. *Tell participants that this course is designed to address the problems that contribute to depression in a predetermined order, which may or may not match the priorities they have assigned in figure 4-1. Confirm that all four skill components will eventually be covered during the course.*

Session 2
How to Design a
Self-Change Plan

Session 2 is devoted to self-change skills. This is the only session in which the instructor presents material that is not covered completely in *Control Your Depression* (some of the issues are discussed in Chapter 6). The instructor thoroughly explains the steps in making a self-change plan: pinpointing, baselining, discovering antecedents and consequences, setting goals, contracting, and choosing reinforcers. By the end of this session it is important for all participants to master the basic procedures for self-change. Understanding these techniques is a prerequisite for subsequent sessions.

AGENDA

    I. BUSINESS
   II. PEP TALK
  III. REVIEW SESSION 1 AND RELATED HOMEWORK
  IV. RATIONALE FOR SESSION 2
   V. LECTURE: SELF-CHANGE SKILLS
  VI. REVIEW SESSION 2 HOMEWORK
 VII. PREVIEW SESSION 3 AND ASSIGN HOMEWORK

I.   **BUSINESS**

II. **PEP TALK** (suggested)

  A. Your expectations are important. It is essential for you to believe that you can change, that you can learn new skills and actually apply them in your daily life.

  B. Your expectations must be kept within realistic limits. If your goals are set too high, then you may become discouraged. Therefore recognize that you have the potential to change, but expect the changes to take place in small, gradual steps.

  C. Your long-term goal is to design your own individually tailored self-change plan. Today we'll lay the groundwork by teaching you some of the basic principles.

  D. This technique may seem artificial at first, but it gets easier and eventually you will see that it's just a more structured way to do what you already do.

  E. Reiterate: It is important to do your homework.

III. **REVIEW SESSION 1 AND RELATED HOMEWORK**

  A. Session 1 review.

   1. Depression is a problem in living.

   2. Three facets of a mutually-interactive system: behavior, thinking, and feeling. Each influences the others.

   3. The two spirals: negative and positive.

   4. Skill building is the focus of this course.

     a. Self-changing skills in general.

     b. Specific skills.
        1) Relaxation.
        2) Pleasant activities.
        3) Constructive thinking.
        4) Social skills.

B. Session 1 homework review.

1. Reminder: do the homework assigned in class, not the homework requested in *Control Your Depression*.

2. Mood monitoring.

a. How do you remind yourself to do it?

b. Any problems assigning a number to mood?

c. If your mood tends to fluctuate, then take an average for the day.

IV. RATIONALE

A. The lecture today will cover some material that is not covered in detail in your textbook. This unit covers the basic skills that are the foundation for the rest of the course. You have already done some of the work by filling out figure 4-1 and assigning priorities to the problems that are contributing to your depression. Today you will learn step-by-step self-change skills you can use to change the problems you have identified. You are encouraged to take notes because it is very important to understand the material presented in today's lecture.

B. Self-control is different from will power. Self-control is a skill that you can learn.

C. There are three critical ingredients for self-change.

1. The belief that you can change.

2. Recognizing that self-change is a skill that you can learn.

3. Developing an action plan.

V. LECTURE: SELF-CHANGE SKILLS

There are seven steps for making a self-change plan:

A. **Pinpointing,** or specifying the problem.

1. Pinpoint a behavior or thought (not a feeling).

2. The behavior or thought must be specific, observable, and countable.

3. It must be something that you want to increase, something that you want to decrease, or some new skill that you want to learn.

B. **Baselining,** or gathering information, keeping track.

1. This is done so that you know where you stand with regard to

48

this particular behavior at the present time. Collecting baseline data allows you to:

  a. Set a reasonable goal for change, and

  b. Keep track of your progress.

2. Count all occurrences of the pinpointed behavior for a certain amount of time (e.g., a week).

3. It is important to count accurately; a portable system for counting can be very helpful (e.g., a 3x5 note card).

4. You not only want to establish how often the behavior is occurring, but also in what situations.

5. By the end of the baselining period, you should know how you want to change the pinpointed behavior and be able to set a reasonable goal.

C. **Discovering antecedents.**

1. Antecedents occur before we engage in a given behavior.

2. Look for conditions that may be related to your pinpointed behavior.

3. There are four types of antecedents.

  a. Social situations.

  b. Your own feelings and thoughts.

  c. Physical circumstances.

  d. The behavior of other people.

4. You can control antecedents in three ways.

  a. Avoid them.

  b. Change them.

  c. Not respond to them.

5. You should try to discover antecedents during the baseline period and then think about possible ways of controlling them.

D. **Discovering consequences.**

1. Consequences are events that happen *after* we engage in a behavior. They affect how we feel about a behavior and the likelihood that we will engage in it again.

49

2. There are two main kinds of consequences.

   a. Reactions from other people.

   b. Our own reactions, that is, the things we say to ourselves.

3. Consequences may be positive (increase likelihood) or negative (decrease likelihood).

4. To increase a behavior, you want the behavior to be followed by many positive consequences and few negative ones.

5. To decrease a behavior, you don't want the behavior to be followed by positive consequences.

6. Think about how you might control consequences (positive and negative).

BREAK

V. **LECTURE** (continued)

   E. **Setting goals.**

   1. It is important to set goals for yourself that are modest and attainable; even a small step in the right direction is significant.

   2. Your goals should be alterable; you are not committed to these particular goals for life.

   3. Increase your goals slowly and only increase them after you have attained a previous goal.

   F. **Contracting.**

   1. Make a specific agreement to reward yourself if and only if you accomplish certain steps toward goals.

   2. Specify clearly the outcome and the consequence.

   3. Timing is very important; reward yourself immediately, if possible.

   G. **Choosing reinforcers.**

   1. In general, reinforcers should:

      a. Make you feel good.

b. Be accessible; otherwise they won't be used.

c. Be powerful; the reinforcers that you receive should be commensurate with the effort that you went through to earn them.

d. Be under your control; don't rely on someone else who may be unreliable.

e. Be as close in time as possible to goal achievement.

2. *It may be helpful to suggest to the participants that they put together a menu listing a variety of reinforcers with their various strengths. A sample is provided in Appendix 6.4.*

VI. DEVELOP A HYPOTHETICAL SELF-CHANGE PLAN

Ask for a volunteer who is willing to share his or her highest priority problem. Use that problem to show the group how to use the steps for developing a self-change plan presented in the lecture. Participants should select a problem from their homework assignments (one of the problems they listed in figure 4-1) for this exercise, but almost any target problem will do. For example, someone might select increasing exercise as a problem to work on. The group can then discuss how to pinpoint the problem, baselining, identifying possible antecedents and consequences, setting goals, contracting, and choosing reinforcers. The purpose of this discussion is to illustrate the principles involved in developing a self-change plan. It is very important for participants to become familiar with these principles because they will be asked to use them in homework assignments throughout the course.

VII. PREVIEW SESSION 3 AND ASSIGN HOMEWORK

A. Preview.

1. Tension gets in the way of doing things that are necessary to overcome depression.

2. Relaxation is a skill that takes practice to develop.

3. Two common procedures are Jacobsen's progressive deep muscle relaxation (which we will do in class next time) and a more portable, passive method developed by Benson (which is described in *CYD*).

51

4. Starting today, you will begin taking baseline data on tension levels; during the next session you will learn to apply the relaxation procedures to see if you can lower your average tension level.

B. *Assign homework. Have students turn to Session 3 in their workbooks. Go over the homework assignment, explaining the relevant tracking forms.*

1. Continue to monitor your daily mood.

2. Read Chapter 5 in CYD.

3. Fill out the Daily Monitoring—Relaxation form each day. Leave the bottom part of the form ("Relaxation Practice") blank—this will be completed when we begin to work on relaxation techniques during the next session.

Session 3
Learning to Relax

Session 3 is an introduction to relaxation training. In this session, the Jacobsen progressive muscle relaxation procedure is presented to supplement the Benson relaxation technique that is outlined in *Control Your Depression*. Excessive and uncontrolled tension can seriously impair an individual's ability to enjoy activities and social interaction and in this way can place an individual at serious risk for depression. It is important for participants to practice these techniques regularly so that they can learn to be relaxed in problem situations. Participants are asked to monitor their tension level and practice a relaxation technique daily.

Recommended Reading:

Benson, H. *The Relaxation Response.* New York: William Morrow, 1975.

Jacobsen, E. *Progressive Relaxation.* Chicago: University of Chicago Press, 1929.

Rosen, G.M. *The Relaxation Book.* Englewood Cliffs, New Jersey: Prentice-Hall, 1977.

AGENDA

   I. BUSINESS
  II. PEP TALK
 III. REVIEW SESSION 2 AND RELATED HOMEWORK
 IV. RATIONALE FOR SESSION 3
  V. LECTURE: PROGRESSIVE RELAXATION
 VI. REVIEW SESSION 3 HOMEWORK
VII. PREVIEW SESSION 4 AND ASSIGN HOMEWORK

*   *   *

I.   BUSINESS

II. PEP TALK (suggested)

   A. **Change.** It can be scary to make changes in your life. The status quo is more familiar, "safer," and easier. However, making changes can also be exciting and very beneficial. This course should be viewed as an opportunity and a challenge to make some changes in your life. We think you will be happy with the results.

   B. **Helping others.** One way to feel better is to reach out to others and try to help them. We hope that in this class you will be supportive, helpful, and understanding with each other. This will not only benefit the other person, but also yourself.

   C. **Process comments.** If you have any comments concerning what is going on in class, this is a good time for discussion.

III. REVIEW SESSION 2 AND RELATED HOMEWORK

   A. Review Session 2: Self-change skills.

     1. Basic self-change skills are the foundation for the course.

     2. There are three essential ingredients for self-change.

       a. The belief that you can change.

54

 b. Recognizing that self-change is a skill that you can learn.

 c. Developing an action plan.

3. Steps for making a self-change plan.

 a. Pinpointing behavior. Define it so that it is specific, observable, and countable.

 b. Baselining. Keeping track of pinpointed behavior (establish how often and in what situations) will help you to set goals and design a strategy for change.

 c. Discovering antecedents. These can be situations, feelings, etc.

 d. Discovering consequences. Classify them as positive, negative, or neutral.

 e. Setting a goal. Make sure that it is reasonable and attainable.

 f. Contracting. Reward yourself if, and only if, you have accomplished your goal.

 g. Choosing reinforcers. They should be accessible, powerful enough, and dispensed with proper timing.

4. These should all be familiar to you by now.

5. You should understand that self-control is not the same as will power.

6. This is an important unit. Are there any questions?

B. Review homework.

1. Even though it is not required, is anyone actually carrying out his or her plan? How successful have you been?

2. *Help trouble-shoot problems.*

IV. RATIONALE

A. Tension gets in the way of overcoming your depression.

1. Tension interferes with enjoying things that you might otherwise enjoy.

2. Tension causes fatigue and tension headaches.

B. Anxiety and tension are survival responses that have evolutionary value; the fight or flight phenomenon is an illustration of this.

1. Modern day dangers and stresses are less tangible than in primitive times; as a result, relaxation is a skill that we need to learn in order to cope effectively with our environment.

2. Relaxation is a skill which can be improved with practice.

3. People are different with regard to how quickly they can learn to relax.

4. Many people do not notice when their muscles are tense; however, the information about muscle tension is available. There are receptors within the muscles that send messages to the brain when a particular muscle is tense. We can think of this as the mind-body connection.

5. Expectations of complete relaxation (i.e., 0 or 1 tension level) are unrealistic. A certain "adaptive level" of tension is necessary in order to function effectively.

C. The relaxation procedures explained here are not hypnosis; they are skills that require a substantial amount of conscious work.

1. The two methods covered in this course are progressive deep muscle relaxation developed by Dr. Jacobsen and a more passive, portable method developed by Dr. Benson.

2. The Jacobsen procedure involves tensing and then relaxing muscles. It is useful because it gives you a running start on relaxation by helping you to notice the difference between relaxed and tense states.

BREAK

V. LECTURE: PROGRESSIVE RELAXATION

A. The Jacobsen progressive deep muscle relaxation procedure.

It is important for participants to understand the rationale for tensing the muscles (e.g., use the analogy of pulling back and releasing a pendulum vs. pushing it, or "getting a running start").

While each individual may have a unique set of tension-producing methods, the following list includes the most commonly used methods. Feel free to experiment and invent different strategies if these methods do not seem to produce sufficient tension. Be sure to let each individual determine which methods work best before you begin the actual relaxation procedure. It will also help to demonstrate the relaxation "patter" briefly so that the participants can become accustomed to it and understand the cue words (the word "NOW" to begin tensing and the word "RELAX" to stop tensing). Each muscle group should be tensed for 5-7 seconds followed by approximately 30 seconds of relaxation. Repeat this procedure once before moving on to the next group of muscles. While tensing the muscles of the feet, the participants should hold the tension for 3-5 seconds rather than the customary 5-7 seconds because cramps may develop quite easily in this area. The muscles in the chest that are associated with deep regular breathing seem to be particularly powerful muscles for inducing generalized relaxation throughout the body and should be referred to periodically after this area has been relaxed.

It is important that your voice reflect the appropriate phase of the tension-release cycle. You should speak somewhat louder and faster, with an element of tension in your voice, during the tension phase. Do not overdo this, however, as it may interfere with participant concentration. A good way to develop this is to tense and relax your own muscles as you go along. Your voice should return to a slow, soft, almost monotone manner of speaking during the relaxation phase. The timing of the tension and relaxation cycles is important and should be practiced with a watch until you can do it accurately. In addition to the difference in voice quality during the tension-release cycle, there should be an overall reduction in the speed and loudness of the voice during the session. Thus, what begins as an almost conversational tone gradually progresses to a slow, almost hypnotic monotone timed to coincide with the participants' breathing. Examples of good "patter" are provided in Rosen (1977) and in Appendix 6.1. After the relaxation procedure is completed, get feedback from the participants regarding their experiences.

1. Tense and relax major muscle groups.

   a. First major muscle group.
      1) Hands and arms—make a tight fist.
      2) Biceps—push down on the arm of a chair with your elbow,

or pull your elbows in toward your body, or bring your forearm up against your biceps.

   b. Second major muscle group.
      1) Forehead—lift your eyebrows or produce a "knit brow."
      2) Upper cheeks and nose—squint your eyes and wrinkle your nose.
      3) Lower cheeks and jaws—clench your teeth and pull back the corners of your mouth.
      4) Neck and throat—pull your chin down or press your neck against the back of the chair.

   c. Third major muscle group.
      1) Chest—take a deep breath and hold it.
      2) Shoulders and upper back—move your shoulders into an exaggerated shrug or touch your shoulders together behind your back.
      3) Stomach—tighten your stomach as if you were going to hit yourself.

   d. Fourth major muscle group.
      1) Thighs—press your heels into the ground or lift your legs slightly off the ground or press your knees together.
      2) Calves—push your toes into the ground or point your toes away from your head or point your toes toward your head.
      3) Feet—turn your feet inward and curl your toes under.

2. *Bring participants back to attention slowly.* Notice your tension level before, during, and after the relaxation exercise on a 10-point scale.

BREAK

V.   LECTURE (continued)

   B. **The Benson procedure.**

     1. Preliminary steps.

       a. Choose a quiet, comfortable environment.

    b. Choose a quiet time of day, for example, two hours after a meal.

    c. Choose a word or phrase to repeat to yourself (e.g., "one").

    d. Develop a passive attitude.

    e. Choose a comfortable position.

  2. Description of the procedure.

    a. Sit quietly in a comfortable position.

    b. Close your eyes.

    c. Progressively relax your muscles.

    d. Breathing—say "one" as you breathe out.

    e. Do this for 10 to 20 minutes—then sit quietly for a few minutes.

VI. REVIEW SESSION 3 HOMEWORK

A. Notice consistencies on relaxation tracking forms. Were there any themes in tracking? Were you consistently tense during certain times of the day or around certain people or in certain situations?

B. Did you have any trouble coming up with an average for the day?

C. Find antecedents for tension.

D. *In small groups or in the whole group, help participants calculate their weekly average tension level for their most relaxed time, their least relaxed time, and their overall average.*

  1. *In small groups, have participants generate their own problem situation lists so that they will be prepared for the next homework assignment.*

  2. *In the whole group, it is suggested that a list of problem situations be listed on the blackboard.*

VII. PREVIEW SESSION 4 AND ASSIGN HOMEWORK

A. Preview: Relaxation in problem situations.

  1. Relaxation skills become particularly important when they are

used before or during anxiety-producing situations. This session is aimed at helping you become more relaxed in general and in specific problem situations.

B. *Assign homework. Have participants turn to Session 4 in their workbooks and follow along. Hold up the monitoring forms to make sure everyone understands.*

1. Continue to monitor your daily mood.

2. Review Chapter 5 in *CYD*.

3. Practice relaxation procedures for at least 30 minutes daily using the Jacobsen procedure, the Benson procedure, or some combination.

4. Evaluate your progress by filling out the entire Daily Monitoring—Relaxation form each day.

5. Complete the Daily Monitoring—Relaxation in Problem Situations form each day.

Session 4
Relaxation in
Everyday Situations

The fourth session is devoted to techniques for applying relaxation strategies in problem situations. Covert and "portable" relaxation techniques are discussed and participants are encouraged to identify their own "tension situations" and to decide in advance which relaxation techniques they will use in those circumstances. The homework involves monitoring tension in problem situations and applying relaxation techniques.

AGENDA

   I. BUSINESS
  II. PEP TALK
 III. REVIEW SESSION 3 AND RELATED HOMEWORK
  IV. RATIONALE FOR SESSION 4
   V. LECTURE: RELAXATION IN EVERYDAY SITUATIONS
  VI. REVIEW SESSION 4 HOMEWORK
 VII. PREVIEW SESSION 5 AND ASSIGN HOMEWORK

I. BUSINESS

II. PEP TALK (suggested)

You have now had a few days to practice using the first skill for controlling depression—relaxation. You have also collected some baseline information about your overall tension level and about tension in problem situations. All of this new input and homework may feel somewhat overwhelming. Don't feel discouraged, try to "hang in there" and keep up the good work.

III. REVIEW SESSION 3 AND RELATED HOMEWORK

A. Review Session 3: Progressive Relaxation.

1. Tension gets in the way of overcoming depression.

2. Anxiety and tension are survival responses with evolutionary value.

3. Relaxation is a skill that takes practice.

4. Two common procedures are Jacobsen's progressive deep muscle relaxation and Benson's relaxation procedure.

5. Students should be practicing one of the relaxation procedures (or a combination of them) daily in order to lower their average daily tension level.

6. Progressive deep muscle relaxation is useful because it allows you to get a running start on relaxation by helping you to distinguish between tension and relaxation states.

7. The Benson procedure is useful because it is portable and less conspicuous.

B. Review homework.

1. How is your relaxation practice going? Any problems? *Stress the importance of regular practice for mastering the skill.*

2. *Check on tracking (Daily Monitoring--Relaxation form). Reinforce successes and trouble-shoot problems.*

62

IV. RATIONALE

Finding out what situations are particularly tension-producing for you is an important step toward using relaxation skills efficiently. After identifying problem situations, you can schedule your relaxation practice to help you approach these situations in a more relaxed mood, or you can use "portable" relaxation techniques when you notice yourself becoming tense.

V. LECTURE: RELAXATION IN EVERYDAY SITUATIONS

Applying relaxation skills in everyday situations requires some creativity.

A. Often it helps to relax yourself before you approach a potentially stressful situation or during the times of day when you tend to be tense.

1. To identify situations that are accompanied by high levels of tension, look at your Daily Monitoring—Relaxation form.

   a. Do your tension levels follow any particular pattern?

   b. Are there specific times of day or situations in which you tend to feel more tense?

2. Try to schedule relaxation practice sessions just before these tension-producing situations. Even a few minutes of practice is better than none.

3. Try imagining yourself acting in a calm manner as you enter a stressful situation.

B. If a stressful situation arises unexpectedly, or if you are otherwise unable to prepare yourself beforehand, a variety of "portable" relaxation techniques may be helpful. It is always easier to control your tension before it becomes too intense. Keep an eye on yourself and try to notice when tension is beginning to increase so that you can intervene as early as possible.

1. Check the tension level of the muscle group where you tend to hold tension. If possible, tense and then relax these muscles.

2. Take a deep breath and exhale slowly while repeating your own relaxation word (e.g., "calm," "one," or whatever).

3. Picture yourself relaxing in your favorite place.

4. Use any cues you can create to help yourself relax.

C. Warning: Changing the way you respond to problem situations takes time, patience, and practice. Don't expect it to work completely or immediately; try to pay attention to any signs of gradual progress.

BREAK

VI. REVIEW SESSION 4 HOMEWORK

Suggestion: Have participants pair up for the following tasks. The instructor should circulate among pairs as a consultant. Afterwards, regroup for a discussion.

A. Note patterns of tension from your Daily Monitoring—Relaxation form.

1. Times of day.

2. Good or bad situations (antecedents).

B. Discuss relaxation practice.

1. Relaxation ratings.

2. Successes or failures.

C. Review your Daily Monitoring—Relaxation in Problem Situations form.

1. Are the problem situations pinpointed enough/too much?

2. Expand your list if necessary.

3. Prioritize the Problem Situations list.

VII. PREVIEW SESSION 5 AND ASSIGN HOMEWORK

A. Preview: Pleasant Activities.

1. The frequency with which you engage in pleasant activities has an impact on depression.

      a. A high frequency of pleasant activities is associated with satisfaction and happiness.

      b. A low frequency of pleasant activities is associated with depression.

      c. We feel good when we do a lot of things that we enjoy.

  2. Plan to work on increasing your participation in pleasant activities and see how it relates to your mood.

  3. Give out personalized lists of pleasant activities.

B. *Assign homework.*

Have participants turn to Session 5 in the workbook. Go over each part of the assignment explaining the relevant forms.

  1. Continue to monitor your daily mood.

  2. Read Chapter 6 in *CYD*.

  3. Practice using relaxation in problem situations and monitor your progress by completing the Daily Monitoring—Relaxation in Problem Situations form each day.

  4. Monitor your daily rate of pleasant activities, using the Activity Schedule.

  5. Graph your mood and level of pleasant activity.

Session 5
Pleasant Activities and Depression

In Session 5 the focus is upon the relationship between pleasant activities and mood. The scores from the "Pleasant Events Schedule" that all participants completed before beginning the course are used to provide each participant with a personalized list of 100 pleasant activities. The procedures for administering and interpreting this inventory are explained in detail on pages 75-95 of *Control Your Depression*. Participants are asked to monitor their enjoyment of and engagement in their particular list of activities; a graph is provided to illustrate the correspondence between the level of pleasant activities and mood.

AGENDA

    I. BUSINESS
   II. PEP TALK
  III. REVIEW SESSION 4 AND RELATED HOMEWORK
  IV. RATIONALE FOR SESSION 5
   V. LECTURE: PLEASANT ACTIVITIES
  VI. REVIEW SESSION 5 HOMEWORK
 VII. PREVIEW SESSION 6 AND ASSIGN HOMEWORK

I.   BUSINESS

II. PEP TALK (suggested)

   A. You can't expect to feel good all of the time. Everyone has his or her bad days. You won't be able to eliminate them completely. It is important for you to set realistic goals ("I want to feel good most of the time" or "I would like to be more in control of my mood"). Depression often results when people set unrealistically high goals. You need to learn to establish limited, achievable goals.

   B. At this point you may find that you are feeling somewhat overwhelmed. That is a natural response to covering a lot of new material. You may not learn every last bit of information that is presented in this course, and that's all right. Everyone is going to work through the course at his or her own pace. The important thing is to stay with it and do your best.

III. REVIEW SESSION 4 AND RELATED HOMEWORK

   A. Review: Relaxation in everyday situations.

      1. By now you have learned to monitor your daily tension level and you have compiled a list of problem situations.

      2. The main idea is to try to schedule relaxation practice before high tension situations occur or to use modified relaxation techniques while those situations are actually taking place.

         a. Take a deep breath and focus on your breathing for a few minutes.

         b. Repeat your special relaxation word to yourself for a couple of minutes.

         c. Picture yourself relaxing in your favorite place.

         d. Relax the muscles that feel the most tense.

   B. Review homework.

      1. Review your Daily Monitoring—Relaxation in Problem Situations form.

2. Note changes in tension levels across the same situations before and after intervention.

3. Reinforce any successes, no matter how small they may be.

4. General questions:

   a. How did you remember to cue a relaxation response?

   b. Which relaxation strategy seemed to work best for you, Jacobsen, Benson, or both? Describe the situations in which you used the relaxation technique(s) and your response. Did you experience the situations any differently?

   c. *Reinforce successes and trouble-shoot problems.*

IV. RATIONALE

A. Research has shown that the rate of pleasant activities and occurrences of depression are reciprocally related. This gives you a powerful tool for learning how to control your depression.

   1. When you are depressed, you are less motivated to do things. This results in a decrease in pleasant activities (and activity level in general).

   2. When your rate of pleasant activities falls below a critical level, you are very likely to become depressed.

BREAK

V. LECTURE: PLEASANT ACTIVITIES

A. People are very different with respect to the specific kinds of activities that they experience as pleasant. However, it has been found that a particular person's pleasant activities are fairly stable over time.

B. There is a subset of pleasant activities that is especially important in determining depression, i.e., mood related activities. These are starred items on the Pleasant Events Schedule.

1. Pleasant social interactions—interactions with others that are experienced as positive and pleasurable (e.g., expressing affection, frank and open conversations with friends).

2. Competency experiences—experiences that make us feel skilled or competent (e.g., successfully learning to do something new, performing a task well).

3. Incompatible responses—activities that are incompatible with feeling depressed (e.g., calling a good friend, sleeping well, laughing, being relaxed).

C. Thousands of people (who were not depressed at the time) have taken the Pleasant Events Schedule. *(Norms are depicted on page 90 of* Control Your Depression. *More extensive norms may be obtained by writing to the senior author).* The information obtained from the Pleasant Events Schedule is scored as follows:

1. Frequency score—how often you engaged in pleasant activities in general at the time of the test.

2. Potential enjoyability score—this is an index expressing how pleasant a particular activity was at the time of the test.

3. Cross-product score—this is a measure of the pleasure obtained from the activities that you were engaged in.

D. Several different patterns.

1. Low frequency/low enjoyability—for this pattern the goal is to work on enjoyability first, then frequency.

2. Low frequency/average or above average enjoyability—for this pattern the goal is to increase the frequency.

3. Average or above average frequency/low enjoyability—for this pattern the goal is to work on increasing enjoyability.

E. Some general antecedents for problems with pleasant activities.

1. Pressure from activities (Type A) that are not pleasant but must be performed (e.g., homework interferes with dancing on Friday night).
Solution: Use time management to make sure that homework is completed before Friday night.

2. Lack of care in choosing activities, resulting in a poor match between what one likes to do and what one actually does (e.g., spend the weekends working around the house instead of going fishing).
Solution: Try to make time for the things you like to do.

3. Sometimes a change will take place that removes the availability of a pleasant event (e.g., someone dies, you move, you get a divorce).
Solution: Work on finding substitute pleasant activities.

4. Anxiety and discomfort interfere with enjoyment (e.g., lack of social skills causes a person to be anxious at parties).
Solution: Identify the source of interference (e.g., tension, lack of social skills) and work on removing it.

VI. REVIEW SESSION 5 HOMEWORK

A. Any problems monitoring pleasant activities each evening?

B. Check pleasant activities graph and activities schedule.

1. *If some people have problems graphing, it is suggested that small groups be formed for additional help in learning techniques for constructing graphs.*

2. Check for patterns between mood and pleasant activities.

3. Does there seem to be a critical number of pleasant activities associated with an acceptable mood score for you?

4. Are there particular activities that seem to have a powerful impact on your mood?

C. *Give PES feedback.*

1. *Hand out PES Score Summary Sheets (see Appendix 6.2).*

2. *Describe each scale and give examples of items in each scale.*

3. *Answer questions.*

4. *Note that the frequency/enjoyability correlation is an indication of how well each participant is doing at engaging in activities that are enjoyable.*

VII. PREVIEW SESSION 6 AND ASSIGN HOMEWORK

A. Preview: Writing a pleasant activities plan.

1. It is important to get started right away on writing a plan for increasing pleasant activities.

   a. Set a goal that strikes a balance between pleasant and unpleasant activities.

   b. Plan ahead by filling out the schedule.

   c. Select activities that are potentially pleasant for you; make sure to select activities that are available.

   d. Set modest goals; an increase of one to five pleasant activities per day over baseline rate is appropriate.

   e. Reward yourself for achieving your goals.

   f. Evaluate your progress.

2. *At this point it may be useful to have the class break into small groups so that participants may help each other set reasonable goals.*

3. *Some participants may experience an increase in their pleasant activities simply as a result of self-monitoring. In this case, a reasonable goal might be to try to maintain this increase in pleasant activities.*

B. *Assign homework.*

1. *Have the students turn to Session 6 in their workbooks.*

2. *Read the goals and the assignment aloud. Suggest using the Weekly Plan form to aid in developing and achieving a pleasant activities plan.*

   a. Continue to monitor your daily mood.

   b. Read Chapter 9 in *CYD* ("Controlling Thoughts").

   c. Formulate a written plan for increasing your daily rate of pleasant activities.

   d. Begin to implement your pleasant activity plan. Evaluate your progress by continuing to monitor your daily rate of pleasant activities on the Activities Schedule.

71

Session 6
Formulating a
Pleasant Activities Plan

Session 6 presents the guidelines for writing a weekly activities plan. The purpose of this plan is to provide a systematic method for increasing and then maintaining the occurrence of pleasant activities at an adequate level. Class participants are encouraged to continue to monitor their activities and mood.

AGENDA

I. BUSINESS

II. PEP TALK (suggested)

One benefit derived from being part of a group is that we can support and help one another. We can help each other learn and make the class enjoyable. Whether or not you maintain the gains that you achieve in class, however, will depend upon your own individual efforts.

III. REVIEW SESSION 5 AND RELATED HOMEWORK

A. Review: Pleasant activities.

1. The number of pleasant activities you engage in is related to your mood.

2. If the number of pleasant activities falls below a critical level, your mood is likely to become increasingly depressed.

3. It is important to achieve a balance between neutral or unpleasant activities, and pleasant activities.

B. Review homework.

1. Any problems monitoring activities?

2. Check graphs. Is there a relationship between mood and pleasant activity level?

3. Have you noticed any changes in your mood since you began to work on increasing pleasant activities?

IV. RATIONALE

A. Pleasant activities give you a "handle" on your mood. You can control your mood by attending to the balance between pleasant activities and neutral or unpleasant activities and by planning to keep your rate of pleasant activities at an adequate level.

B. Goals for this session.

1. To become aware of the impact of specific activities on your daily mood.

2. To work on a self-change plan aimed at increasing pleasant activities. Each of you should have a self-change plan; today we'll go over it and fine-tune it for continued use.

V. LECTURE: MAKING A PLEASANT ACTIVITIES PLAN

A. A good plan is one that you will be able to follow consistently.

B. Objective: To achieve a modest increase in your rate of pleasant activities from baseline level. This can be accomplished by increasing the rate of activities that you have enjoyed before, or by engaging in some new activities.

C. Some general considerations to keep in mind.

1. The following can contribute to a low rate of pleasant activities:

   a. Pressure from outside activities.

   b. Choosing activities that are not highly pleasant.

   c. Excessive anxiety or discomfort can interfere with your enjoyment of pleasant activities.

2. Commitment—You must commit yourself to putting the plan into effect. In order to do this, you must be willing to make choices, establish priorities and rearrange your life a bit.

3. Balance—the goal is to achieve a balance between the things that you must do and the things that you want to do.

4. Planning—try to anticipate any problems or circumstances that might interfere with completing your plan. How will you take care of demands on your time that might prevent you from engaging in pleasant activities?

5. You will achieve a feeling of control over your life to the extent that you stick to your plan. By controlling your time, you are controlling your life.

BREAK

V. **LECTURE** (continued)

D. More specific issues for increasing pleasant activities.

1. Create a balance between Type A and Type B activities.

a. Definition A vs. B.

1) A = neutral or unpleasant. Something you have to do (e.g., housework, errands). This is very individual. One person's Type A might be another person's Type B.

2) B = things you enjoy doing, whether work or play. If you enjoy housework, then that's a Type B activity for you.

b. Achieving a balance is important; this allows you to accomplish the things that you need to do and also insures that you set aside some time to do the things that you truly enjoy.

c. Strategies.

1) Plan to use your time efficiently—set aside blocks of time for Type A activities; engage in Type A activities only at the designated time.

2) Suggestions for planning time.

a) Make a "to do" list.

b) Use a timer.

c) Do the A's really need to be done today?

d) Can other people help with the A's?

2. Planning ahead.

a. Commit yourself to engaging in more pleasant activities.

1) Schedule your pleasant activities at least one day in advance.

2) Don't let yourself back out or give excuses.

3) Specify the time and place.

b. Anticipate problems and try to prevent them (e.g., unplug the telephone, arrange for a babysitter, make dinner reservations).

3. Setting a specific goal.

a. Look at your baseline rate and decide what level would represent a modest increase. Make sure that the increase is reasonable and attainable.

   b. Select a goal and a daily minimum.

   c. Measure the components of your goal—record the number of activities, the number of hours, etc.

   d. Use a weekly plan. Label each activity "A" or "B" so that you can make sure they are balanced.

   e. Self-observe: check off in red the activities you did not do so you can keep track of your progress toward the goal.

   f. If you don't meet your goal immediately, don't worry. Planning ahead takes time and practice, and unexpected things do happen.

   g. You might want to schedule some relaxation time to help make your activities more pleasant.

4. Reward yourself for attaining goals.

   a. Include a contract for rewarding yourself (see Appendix 6.3). This will increase your chances for success.

   b. Use your reward menu (see Appendix 6.4).

   1) Use a point system.

   2) Give yourself small rewards daily; larger rewards should be given for attaining a goal all week.

5. Check your progress—you may want to adjust your plan if it is too ambitious or not ambitious enough.

VI. REVIEW SESSION 6 HOMEWORK

It may be useful to break the class into small groups of two or three participants. The objective is to make a contract to increase pleasant activities. To do this, you will need to:

A. Review baseline data.

B. Set goals.

C. Plan and schedule A and B activities.

D. Anticipate problems and decide on strategies for avoiding them.

VII. PREVIEW SESSION 7 AND ASSIGN HOMEWORK

A. Preview: Thinking and depression.

   1. Two approaches to controlling your thoughts.

      a. Increasing positive thoughts and decreasing negative thoughts.

      b. Constructive thinking: the ABC method.

   2. You will be required to choose one of the two techniques.

B. *Assign homework. Again, have the students open their workbooks and follow along.*

   1. Continue to monitor your daily mood.

   2. Read Chapter 10 in *CYD*.

   3. Continue to implement your pleasant activities plan and evaluate your progress.

   4. Choose which thinking approach you prefer to work with: increasing positive/decreasing negative thoughts, or the ABC method.

   5. Do the assignment for the technique of your choice.

      a. Increasing positive/decreasing negative thoughts (Chapter 9, *CYD*).

         1) Create an inventory of thoughts.

         2) Baseline daily positive and negative thoughts.

         3) Decide which technique to use.

      b. Constructive thinking/ABC (Chapter 10, *CYD*).

         1) Monitor events using the Daily Monitoring form.

            a) Complete sections A, B, C—one sheet each day.

            b) Ignore section D for now.

Session 7
Two Approaches to Constructive Thinking

Session 7 deals with the impact that negative and unconstructive thoughts can have on your mood. Two different approaches to working on cognitions are presented: (1) behavioral methods for increasing positive thoughts and decreasing negative thoughts (e.g., thought-stopping, planned worry time, priming, time projection, etc.), and (2) methods for thinking more constructively (e.g., ABC techniques, automatic thoughts). After being introduced to both methods, participants are asked to choose the technique they prefer and form subgroups to work on the techniques that they have selected. The leader then works as a consultant, encouraging participants to help each other apply the techniques.

Participants seem to naturally choose which of these approaches they prefer. While we have no data on this, it is our impression that thought-stopping is more useful to individuals with obsessive negative or self-critical thoughts; the ABC technique seems more effective for people who tend to overreact to situations or become upset easily.

Recommended Reading:

Ellis, A. & Harper, R.A. *A New Guide to Rational Living.* Hollywood, California: Wilshire Book Company, 1975.

Kranzler, G. *You Can Change How You Feel.* Eugene, Oregon: RETC Press, 1974.

AGENDA

   I. BUSINESS
  II. PEP TALK
 III. REVIEW SESSION 6 AND RELATED HOMEWORK
 IV. RATIONALE FOR SESSION 7
  V. LECTURES: CONTROLLING YOUR THOUGHTS; CONSTRUC-
     TIVE THINKING
 VI. REVIEW SESSION 7 HOMEWORK
VII. PREVIEW SESSION 8 AND ASSIGN HOMEWORK

*   *   *

I. BUSINESS

II. PEP TALK (suggested)

A. You have made it half way through the course. Congratulations! You have learned how to relax and how to monitor and increase your pleasant activities. Techniques for improving your thinking and social skills are yet to come. Keep up the good work.

B. If you're already feeling better that's great. Chances are that the improvement in your mood has a lot to do with what you've been learning in the course. Now is not the time to let up. You need to sample and practice these new skills now, so you can put them to use in the future.

III. REVIEW SESSION 6 AND RELATED HOMEWORK

A. Review: Following a pleasant activities plan.

1. Because pleasant activities are an important "handle" on mood, the main goal is to achieve an increase in your pleasant activities by developing a self-change plan.

2. A balance is needed between Type A and Type B activities.

79

3. Plan ahead by committing yourself to engage in more pleasant activities, anticipating problems, and filling out a schedule.

4. Set a specific goal that represents a modest increase in rate over baseline.

5. Reward yourself for attaining your goals.

6. Evaluate your progress. You may want to adjust the plan if it is too ambitious or not ambitious enough.

B. Review homework. Take out your Pleasant Activities form whether you've done the assignment or not so you can follow along.

1. Did you succeed in carrying out your plans? If not, have the members of the group help you to problem solve. Did you remember to reward yourself?

2. Are there any volunteers who are willing to show their graphs?

a. Is there a noticeable rise in mood, pleasant activities, or both?

b. Is there a noticeable relationship between mood and pleasant activities?

IV. RATIONALE FOR SESSION 7

A. Thoughts can have a profound effect on mood.

B. There are several advantages to working with thoughts.

1. They are always with you.

2. They are under your control.

C. However, these characteristics can sometimes be disadvantages.

1. Thoughts seem automatic and it's easy to take them for granted; you must learn to become aware of them and take them seriously.

2. Thoughts cannot be observed by other people. You must be particularly conscientious when implementing these techniques because only you will know whether you are properly applying what you learn.

D. You will learn two approaches for changing negative thoughts.

1. Techniques for increasing positive thoughts and decreasing negative thoughts.

2. Techniques for developing more constructive thoughts.

E. Today's lecture will cover both approaches.

1. Have you made your decision about which of the two approaches to use? You should already have several days of baseline. Which approach did you choose?

2. If you haven't decided yet, choose one approach after the lecture. We don't want to overburden you with too much at once; you can work on the second approach later if you find that you are interested.

V. LECTURE: CONTROLLING YOUR THOUGHTS

A. Self-assessment of thinking problems.

1. Compute your rate of positive and negative thoughts to decide if you need to work on thoughts (see *CYD*, p. 143). If your ratio is less than 2, then this approach is very important for you. In general, it is very useful for people who tend to think negatively.

2. Identify important thoughts by noticing some of your positive and negative thoughts for a day and writing them down. You can also use the list on pp. 142-143 of *CYD* to help you identify these thoughts.

3. Make a list of positive and negative thoughts on the Inventory of Thoughts form.

4. Place an asterisk (*) next to the thoughts that you think are the most influential in determining your mood.

5. Count your thoughts by keeping a daily tally for several days (baseline). *Counting thoughts is often a problem for participants. Let them know that this counting procedure is somewhat flexible. They don't necessarily have to count every thought that goes through their head. They may want to look at their inventory every hour on the hour or at every meal and simply count the number of positive and negative thoughts that occurred in the preceding time block.*

B. Managing thoughts. *Instructors should give many examples and use the blackboard to illustrate the main points.*

1. Reducing negative thoughts.

    a. Thought interruption. Stop the negative thought by interrupting it with another thought.

      1) Yell "stop!" and then fade the overt word "stop" into a covert word "stop."

      2) Say "I'm not going to think that now" and then fade this to a covert statement.

      3) Employ the rubber band technique. Wear a rubber band on your wrist and snap it whenever you think a negative thought.

    b. Worrying-time schedule. If you need to think about certain negative things, then schedule a time to do so (no more than 30 minutes per day). Limit your negative thoughts to that time period.

    c. Blow-up technique. Take your negative thought to a ridiculous extreme. What is the worst that you can imagine?

2. Increasing positive thoughts.

    a. Priming. Carry 3x5 cards with positive self-statements.

    b. Using cues. Pair positive thoughts with behaviors that occur frequently (e.g., eating or brushing your teeth).

    c. Notice what you can accomplish rather than what you do not accomplish by making a list of daily successes (e.g., getting to work on time).

    d. Positive self-rewarding thoughts. Reward yourself with positive thoughts (e.g., "I did a good job on that").

    e. Time projection. Think forward to an easier time. It is O.K. to feel down; it is becoming demoralized and losing hope that causes problems. Try to imagine a time when your current problem will be gone.

C. Evaluating your efforts. Pay attention to:

1. Antecedents—places, people, time of day.

2. Consequences—are there rewards for thinking negative thoughts?

3. Mental factors—do you punish yourself for thinking positive thoughts? For example, do you tend to label yourself as self-centered or conceited for thinking positive thoughts about yourself?

D. Also pay attention to these self-change elements:

1. Self-reward.

2. Step-by-step change (be realistic).

3. Modeling (imagine how a nondepressed person would think).

4. Self-observation (this helps with self-reinforcement; it gives you a clear picture of how much you're changing).

BREAK

V. **LECTURE** (continued)

E. Constructive thinking.

1. Introduction. This technique is very useful for people who tend to overreact to problems and difficulties. The goal is to change the way you think about problems and difficulties.

2. Some situations that lead many people to overreact.

a. Being rejected by someone.

b. Being disapproved of, or criticized.

c. Feeling unappreciated.

d. Doing more than your share of the work without receiving credit.

e. Failing, making a mistake, or performing poorly.

3. The ABC Method (Albert Ellis, RET) for constructive thinking.

a. There is a strong connection between how you think and how you feel. It may not be what happens to you that causes you to become depressed, but what you tell yourself about what happens.
A = Activating event
B = What you Believe or say to yourself about A
C = Emotional Consequences

b. Learn to identify beliefs and/or attitudes that cause you to overreact: *B*, what you say to yourself about an event, *A*, causes the emotional reaction, *C*.

    c. There are three relatively reliable indicators of nonconstructive self-talk.

       1) Highly evaluative words: should, must.

       2) Catastrophizing words: it's awful, terrible.

       3) Overgeneralizing: I'll never, nobody ever.

    d. Look at your self-talk. Separate constructive or reasonable talk (e.g., I wish, I would have preferred) from nonconstructive talk (e.g., I should have, I would have been smarter to). *Hand out the list of Ellis's 10 major irrational beliefs (see Appendix 6.5).*

    e. The assignment is to track ABC for one situation per day for a week. *Solicit examples from the group.*

    f. Methods for disputing nonconstructive self-talk.

       1) Argue against irrational beliefs or self-talk.

       2) Argue against "should" and "ought" thoughts with "why should I? . . ."

       3) Question words like terrible and awful with "I would have liked, . . ." "But is it really awful? . . ."

       4) Challenge overgeneralizations with "just because this time . . . does it really mean always?"

       5) If you choose this technique you will begin to write down disputing statements for your irrational negative thoughts.

4. Concluding remarks.

    a. Both techniques take practice.

    b. No one is content or happy all of the time.

    c. The idea is to keep negative feelings at a more reasonable level so we can deal with life's difficulties more constructively.

VI. REVIEW SESSION 7 HOMEWORK

    A. *It is suggested that the class participants be divided into two small groups, one for the positive-negative thought approach and one for the ABC method. The instructor should list the group tasks on the blackboard.*

1. The positive-negative thought group tasks are:

   a. Make sure you have an inventory of thoughts. If not, have the members of your group help you to generate a list or give you suggestions about how you can generate one.

   b. Review your baseline data—any problems?

   c. You should choose one technique for decreasing negative thoughts and one technique for increasing positive thoughts and write them down on your tally sheet.

2. The ABC group tasks are:

   a. Review your baseline data—any problems?

   b. Each of you should give an example of at least one ABC sequence. Help each other to problem-solve and discriminate rational from irrational beliefs.

VII. PREVIEW SESSION 8 AND ASSIGN HOMEWORK

A. Preview: formulating a plan for constructive thinking.

   1. We will go over in more detail the steps necessary to take control of your thoughts (i.e., increasing positive thoughts and decreasing negative ones) and we will work on thinking constructively (i.e., the ABC method).

   2. You will become familiar with self-instructional techniques that will help you to "be your own coach."

B. *Assign homework. Ask participants to get out their workbooks and turn to Session 8. Point out that the pleasant activities section is no longer part of the assignment but they can continue with it if they like.*

   1. Continue to monitor your daily mood.

   2. Read Chapter 11 in *CYD*.

   3. Decide whether to use self-instructional techniques.

   4. Do the appropriate thinking assignment.

      a. Utilize the cognitive technique that you have chosen and monitor your progress, or

      b. Dispute your nonconstructive self-talk and complete the Daily Monitoring form each day.

Session 8
Formulating a Plan for
Constructive Thinking

Session 8 presents some additional methods for gaining control over thoughts. Self-instructional techniques and the use of positive self-statements are introduced as supplemental cognitive strategies.

AGENDA

   I. BUSINESS
  II. PEP TALK
 III. REVIEW SESSION 7 AND RELATED HOMEWORK
 IV. RATIONALE FOR SESSION 8
  V. LECTURE: SELF-INSTRUCTION
 VI. SMALL GROUP TASK: POSITIVE SELF-STATEMENTS
VII. PREVIEW SESSION 9 AND ASSIGN HOMEWORK

*   *   *

I.   BUSINESS

II. **PEP TALK** (suggested)

This part of the course should help you realize how much your thoughts can influence your mood, and, we hope, how much you can influence and control how you think.

III. **REVIEW SESSION 7 AND RELATED HOMEWORK**

A. Review: Controlling your thoughts and constructive thinking.

1. Controlling your thoughts.

a. Identify thoughts—keep track of both positive and negative thoughts.

b. Count thoughts—generate a "master list" of your most important thoughts. Keep track of how many positive and how many negative thoughts you have each day (baselining).

c. Manage thoughts.

1) Methods for decreasing negative thoughts.

a) Thought interruption. STOP technique—begin by saying it out loud, then fade to a covert statement such as, "I'm going to stop thinking that now." Rubber band technique—slap your wrist to punish nonconstructive thoughts.

b) Planned worrying time. Confine your worrying to a certain time and place each day.

c) Blow-up technique. Exaggerate your negative thought until it becomes ridiculous and funny.

2) Methods for increasing positive thoughts.

a) Priming. Carry 3x5 cards with positive self-statements.

b) Use cues. Pair positive thoughts with behaviors that occur frequently (e.g., eating, brushing your teeth, answering the telephone).

c) Notice what you accomplish.

d) Positive self-rewarding thoughts (e.g., "I did a good job on that").

e) Time projection. Look forward to a time when a current problem will no longer seem important.

2. Constructive thinking.

   a. The ABC method helps you to focus on how you think about problems and difficulties. The theory is that feelings of being upset come more from what you say to yourself about what happens in your life than from the actual events.
   A = Activating Event
   B = Beliefs or thoughts
   C = Emotional Consequences

   b. Learn to identify beliefs and attitudes that cause you to over-react.

      1) Self-observe by filling out an ABC form when you become upset.

      2) Identify your self-talk. What do you say to yourself?

      3) Identify nonconstructive self-statements.

         a) Overevaluating (should, must).

         b) Catastrophizing (awful, terrible).

         c) Overgeneralizing (always, never).

   c. Dispute nonconstructive statements (e.g., Why should I? Is it really terrible? Am I really always? . . .).

   d. Remember that it's natural and human to feel upset or angry occasionally. This technique will help you be more in control, and allow you to keep these natural feelings at a reasonable level. You will have more choice about how you feel.

3. *Small group task. Have participants who chose the positive/negative technique and those who chose the ABC method go to different parts of the room. If either group seems too large, you might want to divide it into two smaller groups. The following group tasks should be written on the board. The instructor should circulate among the groups and act as a consultant.*

   a. Positive/negative group.

      1) Evaluate your progress.

      2) Talk about which technique you are using, and how.

      3) Determine what seems to work.

      4) Problem-solve.

b. ABC group.

1) Go over your homework forms.

2) Check identification of constructive *vs.* nonconstructive thoughts.

3) Work on disputing statements (section D on the form).

BREAK

IV. **RATIONALE**

Often people know what they should do, and they know it would be effective if they did it, but somehow they seem unable to actually follow through. Self-instruction techniques can be "the missing link" that helps you to actually do the things that you know you should do.

V. **LECTURE: SELF-INSTRUCTION TECHNIQUES**

A. Benefits of internal self-talk.

1. Makes goals more concrete.

2. Focuses attention on the situation at hand.

3. Activates your memory.

4. Has a distancing effect; allows you to be more objective.

5. Helps you to anticipate problems and plan for handling them.

6. Keeps you calm and on track.

7. Provides motivation.

B. Examples (see Chapter 11 in *CYD*).

1. Bad Memory Bill used self-instruction techniques to remind himself to use memory tricks, and to prevent himself from becoming discouraged.

2. High-Expectations Hank used self-instruction techniques to remind himself to keep his expectations more reasonable.

    3. Realistic Rachel used self-instruction techniques to help herself think more constructively.

  C. Using self-instruction.

    1. Understand what you want to accomplish. Be specific.

    2. Understand how you plan to accomplish it.

    3. Write down your instructions.

    4. Practice your instructions.

      a. Do it.

      b. Imagine it.

      c. Imagine someone else doing it.

    5. Modify your self-instructions if necessary.

    6. Make your self-instructions into a routine.

    7. Reward yourself for using self-instructions.

VI. SMALL GROUP TASK: POSITIVE SELF-STATEMENTS

This task can be done either by the whole group or in smaller groups. The comfort and cohesiveness of the group should dictate the size of the group. Have the group help generate a list of positive self-statements for each individual member. Group members should tell each individual good things they have noticed about him or her; each person should write down these comments for future use (priming).

VII. PREVIEW SESSION 9 AND ASSIGN HOMEWORK

  A. Preview: Social skills.

    1. The quality of social interactions is an important factor in determining occurrences of depression.

    2. Many mood-related PES items are social.

    3. Social skill is defined as the ability to obtain reinforcement from other people.

    4. One social skill we will work on is assertiveness (i.e., the ability to express your feelings to others).

B. *Assign homework. Have all participants open their workbooks to Session 9.*

1. Continue to monitor your daily mood.

2. Read Chapter 7 in *CYD*.

3. Develop a list of problem situations that you would like to handle in a more assertive way.

4. Complete the Self-Monitoring of Assertiveness form each day. *(Show participants how to use it.)*

5. Practice assertive imagery for 15 minutes each day, using two situations from your problem list.

Session 9
Social Skills: The Ability to be Assertive

In Session 9 assertiveness is introduced as a useful skill for interacting with others in a direct and rewarding way. Participants are encouraged to provide examples of situations in which they tend to be nonassertive and feel more depressed. Modeling and role playing are used to work on the problem situations presented. The homework assignment for this session requires participants to pinpoint problem situations and practice covert rehearsal of assertiveness.

Recommended Reading:

Alberti, R.E. & Emmons, M.L. *Your Perfect Right.* San Luis Obispo, California: Impact Publishers, 1982.

Bloom, L.Z., Coburn, K., & Pearlman, J. *The New Assertive Woman.* New York: Dell Publishing Company, 1975.

Johnson, S. *First Person Singular.* New York: J.B. Lippincott Company, 1977.

Smith, M.J. *When I Say No, I Feel Guilty.* New York: Dial Press, 1975.

AGENDA

   I. BUSINESS
  II. PEP TALK
 III. REVIEW SESSION 8 AND RELATED HOMEWORK
 IV. RATIONALE AND LECTURE: SOCIAL SKILLS
  V. REVIEW SESSION 9 HOMEWORK
 VI. PREVIEW SESSION 10 AND ASSIGN HOMEWORK

*   *   *

I.   BUSINESS

II. PEP TALK (suggested)

    A. I would like to begin by reminding you that it's O.K. to reward yourself when you are depressed. We are frequently too hard on ourselves. We tend to set perfectionistic goals and punish ourselves for not achieving them. Modest goals are the rule. For example, making a good effort is often a reasonable goal. It's O.K. to create your own rewards for achieving your goals (e.g., "If I finish this assignment, I'll go to the movies"). We often work for external rewards (e.g., paychecks). Another important source of rewards is what we tell ourselves (i.e., our internal dialogue).

III. REVIEW SESSION 8 AND RELATED HOMEWORK

    A. Review: Formulating a plan for constructive thinking.

       1. You learned how to increase positive thoughts and how to decrease negative thoughts.

       2. Your thoughts can be more constructive if you identify ABC's and replace nonconstructive self-talk with constructive self-talk.

       3. Self-instructional techniques or "being your own coach."

         a. Be specific about what you want to accomplish.

93

      b. Be specific about how you plan to accomplish it.

      c. Write down your instructions.

      d. Practice your instructions by doing them, imagining them, or imagining someone else doing them.

      e. Modify your self-instructions if necessary.

      f. Build self-instructions into a routine.

      g. Reward yourself for using self-instructions.

B. Review homework. Any questions, problems, or comments regarding the material that we have covered on controlling your thoughts?

    1. Did your negative thoughts decrease and positive thoughts increase?

    2. Was anyone able to avoid overreacting to situations that may have resulted in overreactions in the past?

    3. Is anyone using self-instructional techniques? Are they helpful?

IV. RATIONALE AND LECTURE: SOCIAL SKILLS, THE ABILITY TO BE ASSERTIVE

A. Many mood-related activities involve social interactions.

    1. Social skill is the ability to interact with other people in such a way that it is experienced as reinforcing.

    2. There is no "right" way; we must all interact with other people in a manner that will make us feel comfortable. We all have a slightly different "style" of obtaining positive responses from others.

B. Typical social-skill problems of depressed people.

    1. They tend to be less active in social situations.

    2. They find it hard to initiate contact with new people.

    3. They are less comfortable in social situations.

    4. They are more sensitive to being ignored or rejected.

    5. They are less assertive (e.g., they don't stick up for themselves; they don't say what they are thinking).

C. Assertiveness. *(Recommend Manuel Smith's book,* When I Say No I Feel Guilty.*)*

1. Assertiveness is the ability to express your thoughts and feelings openly (e.g., complaints and affections).

2. Assertiveness is important for a number of reasons.

   a. It can facilitate developing close, warm relationships.

   b. It can help to prevent aversive encounters.

   c. It can give you the means for obtaining more positive responses from others.

   d. It allows other people to understand you better.

BREAK

IV. **RATIONALE AND LECTURE** (continued)

D. A plan for working on assertiveness.

1. Develop a Personal Problem List *(CYD,* pp. 112-113) of five to ten problems that meet the following criteria:

   a. A situation that you are currently handling in a nonassertive way.

   b. A situation that occurs regularly in your life (at least once each month).

   c. A situation that is troubling to you.

   d. A situation that strikes a good balance between being too specific and too general.

   e. The situations should be different enough from each other so that you are listing diverse situations and behaviors (unless there is only one problem area).

2. Monitor your assertiveness *(CYD,* p. 113). Track (baseline) assertiveness and comfort levels in your problem situations (0-10 for comfort, and 0-10 for skill).

3. Practice assertive imagery. The goal is to handle situations as well as you can and to feel good about how you handle them.

      a. Practice for at least 15 minutes per day.

      b. Use two easy situations, two situations that are most likely to occur, or two random situations.

      c. Create vivid images.

      d. Use the same scene, but change the details.

      e. Include a vivid image, an assertive statement, and a subsequent response.

    4. Transfer from imagery to real life.

      a. Start with an easy situation.

      b. Plan the situation.

    5. Evaluate your progress.

      a. Try two more situations.

      b. Be more flexible about real life situations.

E. Possible reasons for lack of progress.

    1. A long history of being nonassertive.

    2. Lack of consistent practice.

    3. Standards that are too high.

F. Remember the main steps for self-change.

    1. Set specific goals.

    2. Use small steps.

    3. Monitor your behavior.

    4. Reward yourself for small gains.

G. Other social skills are also important. Ask yourself how you appear to others. (*CYD,* p. 120 lists behaviors that have a negative impact on others.)

    1. A general approach for obtaining positive feedback from others.

      a. Compliment others when appropriate.

      b. Express agreement when you agree.

      c. Keep the conversation going.

        1) Ask questions.

        2) Relate common experiences.

        3) Give an opinion.

2. You need to be willing to take risks and to make mistakes. Reward yourself for taking risks and the level of effort you put forth, not just for successes.

H. When moving to a new social environment, you need to learn to gather information and act on information about social activities. *(Recommend Johnson, S.,* First Person Singular, *for further reading).*

1. Get a local newspaper—read the activities and entertainment section.

2. Ask the Chamber of Commerce for information.

3. Be willing to make a lot of mistakes and waste a few weekends.

4. Call someone—explain the situation and ask for advice.

5. Spend some weekends exploring. Get a map and make a list of the good places that you find.

6. Join a group that does things that you are interested in.

V. REVIEW SESSION 9 HOMEWORK
Ask participants to take out the Self-Monitoring of Assertiveness form (whether or not they have done the assignment).

A. Any problems developing a personal problem list?

B. Any problems monitoring on the assertiveness form?

C. How is the assertive imagery practice going?

D. *If the members of the group are fairly comfortable with each other, it is suggested that the group as a whole be involved in the following exercise:*

1. *Have the group generate a list of problems and put them on the blackboard.*

2. *Pick two or three problem situations that seem to be common (including at least one positive assertiveness situation).*

3. *Use the group to help generate or role play appropriate assertive responses.*

VI. PREVIEW SESSION 10 AND ASSIGN HOMEWORK.

A. Preview: Using your social skills.

1. Many depressed people have good social skills but for various reasons aren't using them.

2. Evaluate your level of social participation using Table 8-1 in *CYD*.

3. It is possible that social participation problems are due to inadequate stimulation or inadequate reward.

   a. Inadequate stimulation means falling into a routine that doesn't provide you with opportunities for doing things with other people.

   b. Inadequate reward means that the social interaction is not rewarding in and of itself.

B. *Assign homework. Have participants take out their workbooks and turn to Session 10. Read the goals and the assignment for Session 10. Be sure to demonstrate how to use each form.*

1. Continue to monitor your daily mood.

2. Read Chapter 8 in *CYD*.

3. Practice assertiveness in real life situations and monitor your progress on the Self-Monitoring of Assertiveness form.

4. Complete the Social Activities Questionnaire.

5. Complete the Social Activities to Increase form.

6. Complete the Interferences: Activities to Decrease form.

7. Develop and carry out a plan for increasing pleasant social activities and monitor your progress. (The plan for increasing social activities should be written out in a few sentences that specify pinpointed activities, goals, and rewards.)

Session 10
Using Your Social Skills

Session 10 introduces the idea that a low rate of social interaction often indicates that there is *inadequate stimulation* (e.g., you get in a rut, you are out of the habit of being around others), and *inadequate reward* (e.g., because of tension, nonassertiveness, or some other difficulty, social activity is no longer rewarding). Participants discuss activities they may need to increase (e.g., calling friends to suggest getting together), and activities they need to decrease (e.g., watching television) in order to increase their level of pleasant social interaction. Specific plans are then developed for increasing social activities and decreasing interfering activities.

AGENDA

    I. BUSINESS
    II. PEP TALK
    III. REVIEW SESSION 9 AND RELATED HOMEWORK
    IV. RATIONALE FOR SESSION 10
    V. LECTURE: USING YOUR SOCIAL SKILLS
    VI. REVIEW SESSION 10 HOMEWORK
    VII. PREVIEW SESSION 11 AND ASSIGN HOMEWORK

I. **BUSINESS**

II. **PEP TALK** (suggested)

As we approach the end of the course, we hope that you feel that you have more control over your mood than ever before. You should be finding out that the skills you have learned here are relatively easy to apply within the context of your daily life. It should also become apparent that by making use of what you have learned, episodes of depression can be minimized or prevented altogether.

III. **REVIEW SESSION 9 AND RELATED HOMEWORK**

A. Review: Social skills.

1. Many mood-related activities involve social interaction.

2. Social skill is the ability to interact with other people in such a way that it is experienced as reinforcing.

3. Assertiveness is the ability to express one's thoughts and feelings openly. Assertiveness is an important skill for developing close, warm relationships.

B. Review homework.

1. Did you fill out the Self-Monitoring of Assertiveness form?

2. Did anyone try out assertive responses? How did it go (comfort, skill)?

3. Did practicing assertive imagery help?

4. What problems did you have? *Take some time here to discuss and to trouble-shoot problems. Allow the group to participate in problem solving.*

IV. **RATIONALE**

Many depressed people have good social skills but for various reasons aren't using them. Sometimes this happens because they have become isolated, or because they have moved and not yet made good friends. This session is designed to help you overcome the problems that prevent you from using the social skills that you have.

The first step is to evaluate yourself. Table 8-1 in *CYD* will help you to evaluate your level of social participation. This evaluation takes into account how comfortable you are socially and how frequently you engage in social activities. Relaxation skills can be useful if your comfort score is low. Today we will concentrate on improving the frequency of social activity.

V. LECTURE: USING YOUR SOCIAL SKILLS

There seem to be two main problems: inadequate stimulation and inadequate reward.

A. Inadequate stimulation occurs when you fall into a routine that doesn't provide you with opportunities to do things with other people. The solution is to break out of the routine.

1. Make a list of potentially enjoyable activities that you seldom do ("social activities to increase"). You might use your list of pleasant activities to give you some ideas. Newspapers can also be a good source of ideas for activities.

2. List the habits you've developed that interfere with participating in social activities with others ("interferences" or "activities to decrease"). What are some habits that might be interferences?

3. Establish goals for increasing social activities and decreasing interferences.

4. Experiment to find a balance that makes you feel good.

B. Inadequate reward occurs when social activities become so unrewarding that you do not enjoy them and do not seek them out.

1. Again, we emphasize the importance of rewarding yourself, especially when you are trying to change your behavior.

a. Reward will provide a boost to get you going.

b. Be sure to reward yourself even if your attempt doesn't work. It is important to reward yourself for trying. (It's often necessary to make several mistakes a week when you are trying something new.)

2. Social interaction should become rewarding once you get started.

3. If this is not the case, and social interaction does not feel good to you, then you'll need to determine why.

   a. Are you too tense? Try relaxation.

   b. Do you have poor social skills? See Chapter 7 in *CYD*; practice assertiveness and other social skills.

BREAK

V. **LECTURE** (continued)

C. General guidelines.

   1. Decrease the amount of time spent engaging in interfering activities.

   2. Gather information about available social activities; try some new ones.

   3. Set reasonable goals that contain small steps.

   4. Reward yourself for achieving small steps.

   5. Give your plan enough time to work. Look for signs of gradual progress.

VI. **REVIEW SESSION 10 HOMEWORK**

A. *Have students take out their Social Activities to Increase and Interferences to Decrease forms.* Does everyone have a list on both forms?

B. What kinds of interferences did you come up with? Do you have strategies for how you're going to decrease them?

C. What kinds of social activities do you want to increase? Did you set daily goals? Weekly goals?

D. *Small group task: Divide the class into groups of two or three participants and go over the monitoring forms. Each of you should have a goal for activities to decrease and activities to increase. Work* on strategies for decreasing interferences and increasing social activities. Decide on appropriate rewards for attaining your goals.

VII. PREVIEW SESSION 11 AND ASSIGN HOMEWORK

A. Preview: Maintaining your gains.

1. Session 11 is very important. In Session 11 we begin to review what we have learned, decide which areas still need the most work, and start to plan how to maintain the gains we have made so far. The plan should include guidelines for continuing to work on problem areas.

B. *Assign homework. Have participants take out their workbooks and turn to Session 11.*

1. Continue to monitor your daily mood.

2. Read Chapter 12 in *CYD:* Maintaining Your Gains.

3. Complete the Beck Depression Inventory (pp. 13-17 or 213-215 in *CYD*). Compare your current score with your score before the course started. *Instructors should hand out previous scores.*

4. Assign priorities to your problems and the methods for coping with them by completing the ratings in the Integration section of Chapter 12 in *CYD* (pp. 178-180). Decide what you can do on a continuing basis to work on these problems.

5. Develop an "emergency plan" that will allow you to anticipate and deal with stressful situations when they occur in the future (see *CYD*, pp. 181-184).

Session 11
Maintaining Your Gains

Session 11 is devoted to summarizing the course material and helping participants to start developing a plan to maintain their gains. Participants review each problem area that was covered in the course and determine which specific areas are still problems for them. Participants then evaluate the techniques that they have learned and select the ones that they would like to continue to use on a regular basis. By the end of the session, participants should have personalized plans to help them continue working on problem areas and deal with "emergency situations" that might arise and cause depression.

AGENDA

    I. BUSINESS
    II. PEP TALK
    III. REVIEW SESSION 10 AND RELATED HOMEWORK
    IV. RATIONALE FOR SESSION 11
    V. LECTURE: MAINTAINING YOUR GAINS
    VI. REVIEW SESSION 11 HOMEWORK
    VII. PREVIEW SESSION 12 AND ASSIGN HOMEWORK

I. BUSINESS

II. PEP TALK (suggested)

Feeling better during the eight weeks of the course is important. More important, however, is what happens after the course ends. You should be actively planning ahead now so that you will maintain the gains that you have achieved and continue to use the skills that you've learned in the course.

III. REVIEW SESSION 10 AND RELATED HOMEWORK

A. Review: Using your social skills.

1. Many depressed people have good social skills but for various reasons aren't using them.

2. Table 8-1 in *CYD* will help you evaluate your level of social participation.

3. Methods of overcoming social participation problems due to inadequate stimulation.

a. List Social Activities to Increase.

b. List Interferences—Activities to Decrease.

c. Intervene—set modest goals for increasing social activities and decreasing interfering activities.

d. Experiment to find a comfortable balance.

4. Methods of overcoming social participation problems due to inadequate reward.

a. Reward yourself.

b. Intrinsic rewards will eventually take over.

c. If social participation does not become intrinsically rewarding it may be because:

1) You are too tense; try relaxation techniques.

2) You have poor social skills (see Chapter 7 in *CYD*); practice assertiveness and/or other social skills.

B. Review homework.

   1. Any questions, problems, or comments regarding the social skills sessions?

   2. Is anyone trying assertiveness?

   3. Is anyone still working on increasing social activities?

IV. RATIONALE

A. Now we have completed the skill components of the course and it is time to plan for the future by reviewing what you have learned and begin working on a "life plan."

B. You will be continuing on your own to practice and apply the skills that you have learned.

C. It is important to see the end of the course as the beginning of your "life plan."

V. LECTURE: MAINTAINING YOUR GAINS

A. Review the material already covered.

   1. Depression is viewed as a problem in living that is characterized by dysphoria, low level of activities, problems interacting with others, guilt, physical problems, and anxiety.

   2. The three-facet model of depression. We have covered skills for each facet.

      a. Thinking: positive/negative thoughts and the ABC method.

      b. Behaving: pleasant activities, assertiveness, and social skills.

      c. Feeling: relaxation and mood.

B. A review of what you have achieved by participating in the course.

   1. Most of you have experienced a decrease in your level of depression.

      a. Compare your score on the Beck Depression Inventory (BDI) that you filled out in *CYD* at the beginning of the course with your more recent scores on the same inventory.

b. If you would like to share the changes that you have noticed in your BDI scores with the group, please feel free to do so.

c. If your scores have not decreased, don't give up. Some participants have experienced a delayed reaction to the course. Keep refining the skills that you have learned in the course until they work for you.

2. A better understanding about the symptoms of depression.

3. The ability to recognize depression in yourself.

4. A greater awareness of the situations, behaviors and thoughts that can cause depression.

5. The ability to design and implement a self-change plan.

BREAK

V. LECTURE (continued)

C. Methods for maintaining your gains.

1. Take time to integrate what you've learned.

a. What contributes to your depression?

b. Assign priorities to your problem areas (refer to Table 12-1 in *CYD*).

c. Describe your methods of coping with your problem areas.

d. Decide how to remind yourself to use intervention strategies if you feel yourself becoming depressed again.

2. Monitor your mood on a regular basis. This is extremely important.

a. Prevention is far easier and less painful than treatment.

b. Try to recognize the early signs of depression.

3. Suggestions.

a. Complete the BDI every month (use a monthly cue to remind yourself, such as receiving your phone bill or paycheck).

b. If you find yourself becoming depressed, go back and use the techniques that worked best for you.

D. Major life events and life changes that often lead to depression.

    1. Situational changes can change the positive outcomes of your behavior and can change the quality of your interactions.

    2. Possible life events that may lead to depression (*CYD,* pp. 181-182):

       a. Social separations.

       b. Health related problems.

       c. New responsibilities and adjustments.

       d. Work-related events.

       e. Financial and material changes.

    3. Major events happening to those close to you can also affect you; they might begin to act differently toward you (e.g., be available less often, less sympathetic, and so on).

    4. Life events do not necessarily have to be negative to cause distress and/or depression (e.g., moving, promotion, graduation).

E. Anticipate and plan for stressful life events.

    1. Anticipate specific ways in which the stressful life event will affect your behavior and your interactions.

    2. Prepare for stressful events by developing a self-change plan.

    3. Observe your depression level more closely during stressful times.

BREAK

VI. REVIEW SESSION 11 HOMEWORK

A. Go over Table 12-1 in CYD *in one of two ways:*

    1. Generate group discussion about each problem area. Encourage the participants to specify how each area applies to their plan for working on high-priority problem areas.

    2. Go around the table or take volunteers. Have participants discuss their high-priority problem areas and present their plans for continuing to work on those areas.

3. It is important for each participant to contribute to the discussion.

B. Generate emergency plans.

1. Do you have an emergency plan?

2. What kinds of stresses are you anticipating? (One potential life change is the end of the course.)

3. What specific strategies do you plan to implement?

VII. PREVIEW SESSION 12 AND ASSIGN HOMEWORK

A. Preview: Developing a Life Plan.

1. The next session will help you think about who you are and who you might become.

2. We will discuss how to plan the direction in which you would like to change and provide guidelines for developing a strategy to help these changes take place.

B. *Assign homework. Have participants take out their workbooks and follow along. Read the goals and assignments for Session 12.*

1. Continue to monitor your daily mood.

2. Read Chapters 13 and 14 in *CYD*.

3. Carefully review the Life Plan form in your workbook. Notice that parts of the Life Plan have already been included in the maintenance plan (*CYD*, Table 12-1, pp. 178-180) and the role sketch (*CYD*, Figure 13-2, p. 191). The Life Plan does not have to be perfect. The point is to write something down so that you can refer to it in the future.

Session 12
Developing a Life Plan

This final class session is devoted to discussing how to develop a meaningful Life Plan. Participants should follow the guidelines in CYD for evaluating their values, goals, and personal styles. Prior to this class session, participants should have pinpointed their problem areas and made plans for continuing to work on them. Some participants may be somewhat reluctant to share their Life Plans with the group, perhaps because of a lack of confidence in their ability to produce a good plan. The instructor should allow individuals to maintain as much privacy as they prefer, but still make sure that each participant has developed a workable Life Plan.

Many final sessions involve a discussion of treatment gains, and "testimonials" are relatively common. Participants who have not achieved significant improvement in their depression level during the course may find this to be a difficult session. The leader should be sure to emphasize that further improvement and maintenance of gains is likely to occur if participants continue to use the coping skills that they have learned in the course. Some people will require additional help in mastering these skills. Some may also find that alternative forms of treatment are necessary. It is the leader's responsibility to discuss plans for the future with members of the group who continue to be depressed; in some cases it may be necessary to provide referrals for more intensive forms of treatment.

AGENDA

   I. BUSINESS
  II. PEP TALK
 III. REVIEW SESSION 11 AND RELATED HOMEWORK
 IV. RATIONALE FOR SESSION 12
  V. LECTURE: MAKING A LIFE PLAN
 IV. REVIEW SESSION 12 HOMEWORK
VII. FINAL PEP TALK, CLOSING REMARKS

*　*　*

I.   BUSINESS
Set the time for a one-month reunion.

II. PEP TALK (suggested)
Because this is the last regular weekly meeting, we will be focusing on the future. We expect that many of you have noticed that you have made significant gains in your ability to improve your mood. Of course, your mood will always fluctuate. There will be times when you feel up and times when you feel down—that is simply part of being human. However, all of you should now have some skills that you can use to prevent depression, or to help yourself feel better if you do become depressed. We hope that you will continue to use these skills.

III. REVIEW: MAINTAINING YOUR GAINS

    A. Carrying out regular assessments of your state of well-being will allow you to recognize the beginning stages of depression so you can work on feeling better.

    B. Anticipate life changes and the impact that they will have on you; design an emergency plan.

    C. Identify your own individual problem areas and the techniques for dealing with them.

    D. Prevention is easier and less painful than treatment.

111

IV. RATIONALE

This is an opportunity for you to think about who you are and who you might become. Plan the direction in which you would like to change.

V. LECTURE: MAKING A LIFE PLAN

A. Often people are afraid to change. Some reasons for this include:

1. Fear of breaking away from the status quo.

2. Fear of inconsistency.

3. Fear that change is an admission of failure.

4. Fear of losing spontaneity. (We become spontaneous by choosing well and wisely, not by refusing to make choices.)

5. Fear of experimenting. Making changes can be exciting, particularly when the changes are planned. You can choose to make changes.

B. Creating yourself. There is no one good way to be. We have suggested that you create a role sketch for yourself that includes goals, style, types of relationships, and values. Describe who you are and "improve" that by suggesting some possible modifications. Describe the changes that you will need to make to become an "improved" person.

C. Maintaining your gains. People often react to a crisis by putting new ideas into practice, but when the crisis passes they return to their old patterns. To prevent this, we want to emphasize:

1. Think preventively, in terms of positive mental health.

2. Learn to recognize and make room for "high points" in your life.

a. Plan for positive mental health. Try not to wait until you already feel bad and then plan to do something about it.

b. Try to view changes as opportunities for growth rather than as threats to your well-being.

D. Effective planning also involves harmonizing your values and your goals.

1. Values are general principles or guidelines that you consider worthwhile.

2. Goals are specific ends toward which you direct your efforts.

   a. Your goals take their meaning from your values.

   b. It is good to deliberately arrange social support systems that reinforce and strengthen your values and goals.

   c. Goals fall into several categories.

      1) Individual goals: life-style (your "image"), economic pursuits, educational plans, vocational choices, physical activity level, spiritual beliefs, recreational and creative activities.

      2) Interpersonal goals: family life-style, sharing time with friends, developing romantic relationships, making group commitments, and assuming leadership roles.

      3) Short-term vs. long-term goals.

      4) Superordinate goals give meaning to life.

E. Design your Life Plan using the form in your workbook.

   1. It is based on your role sketch, goals, and philosophy of life.

   2. It should take into account your identified problem areas.

   3. It should include both short- and long-term goals.

   4. It is a document that provides a reference point for guidance. It can be changed and modified as you change and grow.

   5. It should include an emergency plan—reminders to help you through an expected or unexpected crisis.

BREAK

VI. REVIEW SESSION 12 HOMEWORK

A. *Ask if participants are willing to share their Life Plans. Provide an opportunity for each participant to share his or her material with the group. It may seem appropriate to break into small groups to discuss Life Plans. Some participants may also want some consultation. Use your judgment as to the best way to make sure that everyone has a workable Life Plan.*

B. Review your Life Plan.

    1. Outline your most critical problem areas and ways to continue to work on them.

    2. Design a way to check your depression level regularly.

    3. Consider what you need to change to be more the way you'd like to be.

    4. Outline your goals, both long term and short term.

    5. Keep in mind your philosophy of life and superordinate goals.

VII. FINAL PEP TALK AND CLOSING REMARKS

This is an important pep talk to tailor to the participants. The content of the pep talk is probably less important than the process itself. The issues to address are: Do the participants have a sense of hope and optimism? Are their goals specific and realistic? Do they have a sense of clarity about what they've learned? Have they had a chance to share their feelings about the class experience? Is there a sense of closure?

A. Beginnings and endings are important times. Among other things they provide an opportunity to plan and reflect.

B. We have formed a cohesive, supportive group, and probably each of us depends on the group and its regular meetings in some way. Perhaps you should expect somewhat of a let-down as the course ends, and therefore plan what you can do to deal with that. For instance, you might want to attend carefully to your rate of pleasant activities, particularly social activities.

Close with some remarks about having enjoyed the group, being proud of participants' progress, and so on. Allow time for others to make comments if they wish, and come to a sense of closure.

FOLLOW-UP SESSIONS

Participants return for meetings one month and six months after the last session. These gatherings usually tend to have a more social "reunion" flavor than regular class sessions. Despite this, however, the leader should be sure to check with participants about their progress concerning depression, whether or not they are continuing to use coping skills that were taught in the course, and to reinforce successes. Again, the importance of active maintenance and prevention should be underscored.

Chapter 7

Dealing with Monopolizers and Nonparticipators

This chapter has been included to provide instructors with guidelines for recognizing and dealing with individual differences in participation level among class members. Within any group there are some participants who tend to dominate and others who tend to recede into the background during group interaction. Such diversity in participation level is a natural consequence of combining a variety of personalities into a group. In order for all class members to derive maximum benefit from the Coping with Depression course, however, it is essential for everyone to have an equal chance to participate in group activities. Even though the "equal time" ground rule directly addresses the issue of participation level, it is usually necessary to take additional measures to bring this about. Class members whose level of participation falls at either end of the spectrum (i.e., "Nonparticipators" and "Monopolizers") require special attention from the instructor. In this chapter four types of nonparticipators and four types of monopolizers are described; suggestions are given for dealing with each type of participant.

Monopolizers

"Monopolizers" become a problem when they dominate the group to the extent that less assertive members lose opportunities to participate in the dialogue of the class. Thus, while active talkers may be an asset in a group by keeping the discussion lively and asking useful questions, they may also have an undesirable effect on the interactional dynamics of the group.

The Tangential Talker

"Speaking of pleasant activities...has anyone seen that new movie at Cinema World? I went to see it with my wife last weekend. It was a terrific movie...."

This type of participant tends to lure the group away from the agenda with lengthy discussions about material which is, at best, only loosely related to the topic of the class. For many participants class meetings are an opportunity to interact with relatively congenial and nonthreatening people and to meet potential friends. While it is desirable for the group to become a congenial and cohesive unit, the most important priority is to teach the various skills that members will use to control their depression. Because excessive "social" talk interferes with this goal, it is important to place constraints on runaway tangential talkers.

A.A. is a 47-year-old housewife with grown children who is currently experiencing a major episode of depression. She has been an active and friendly participant in a generally talkative group. At least once during each class session, however, A.A.'s contribution to the group discussion stretches into a lengthy monologue about a family activity, gardening practices, the best way to recycle bottles, or some other unrelated topic. The other group members are too polite to interrupt although they are often visibly bored during her monologues.

Although it would be easy for the group instructor to fall into the role of rule enforcer, this is not the most desirable solution to the problem. In the case of A.A., the instructor found it helpful to periodically remind group members of the equal time ground rule, and asked them to share the responsibility for enforcement. This approach gave group members permission to discourage excessive talkers. It also gave them an opportunity to practice assertive behavior and to enhance their sense of control over their social environment. In this case, A.A. was very responsive to peer pressure and she gradually reduced her tangential talking to an acceptable level.

The Task-Oriented Monopolizer

"Those suggestions might help, but I'm still concerned that they won't completely solve my particular problem. You see...."

A participant who readily offers examples to illustrate the material discussed in the course and who freely brings up problems encountered in carrying out the homework assignments is a welcome member of the group. However, enthusiastic participants can also become a liability if they have a tendency to dominate group interaction. There are several subspecies of the task-oriented monopolizer: the "yes—but" talker, the person with more problems or more important problems than anyone else, and the person who has experienced everyone else's problems and knows the solutions. All share a tendency to remain the focus of attention; typically, their contribution to a discussion is appropriate in content, but inappropriate in duration.

> B.B. is a woman in her mid-forties; she is neatly groomed, overweight, and appears younger than her age. Although she seems somewhat unsure of herself, she is an active participant in her group. B.B. is compulsive about doing her homework assignments, but she often has difficulty understanding and applying the material. The group is characteristically eager to help her understand the material and to assist her in solving the problems she encounters; in addition, her examples and difficulties often provide an excellent opportunity for the group leader to illustrate an elusive point or to work through a common problem. However, it is increasingly clear to the instructor that B.B. is becoming the main focus of each session, the "problem child" of the group, and that other participants are volunteering their own concerns less often.

As in the previous example, the equal time ground rule is being violated. The instructor should encourage discussion concerning the topic for the session but at the same time should try to make sure that all members of the group have a chance to contribute to the discussion. The strategy for dealing with B.B. was to reinforce B.B.'s enthusiasm and involvement with the task, while suggesting a more equal sharing of group "air time." In this particular situation the instructor found that it was productive to work with B.B. so that she discovered her *own* solutions to her problems with the material. By making use of her own resources she was able to reduce her role as "problem child." Because B.B. was no longer placed in the position of listening to (and often rejecting) the suggestions of others, her discussion of her difficulties became shorter and more to the point. On occasions when too much time was still being taken by B.B., the instructor found it necessary to simply interrupt her and move the discussion on to other matters.

The Depressive Talker

> "I had a terrible week, and consequently I couldn't even begin to do the reading assignment. On Monday my daughter's teacher called to complain about her behavior in class. On Tuesday morning the car broke down, and that really got my day off to a great start...."

It is relatively common for depressed persons to talk at length about their problems and about how difficult their lives are. People around them often reinforce this behavior by listening attentively and sympathetically. The "no depressive talk" ground rule is intended to place constraints on the natural tendency toward depressive talk. A depressive talker who is persistent can make the class an unenjoyable and draining experience by encouraging others to view the world in a negative light.

> C.C. is a 43-year-old mail carrier with a rather gloomy demeanor. The quietest member of a rather lively group, he has a tendency to come late to class and not to complete homework assignments. He rarely participates voluntarily in group interaction; however, when a question is directed to him, he seems to take advantage of the opportunity to speak. C.C.'s contribution is usually a lengthy monologue about how bad he feels, how tired he always is, and how he just can't seem to get motivated to do the homework assignments. The group tends to listen patiently, offer sympathy, and occasionally make suggestions to C.C. It is apparent to the instructor, however, that these depressive monologues are not leading to any productive outcome, and that some group members seem to be getting impatient with C.C. and are beginning to seem less enthusiastic about the class.

This particular monopolizer can have a devastating effect on the group. It is often a participant's worst fear that the group will be composed of such members, and that classes will be depressing sessions for "airing your negative feelings." Therefore, depressive talk is not only unconstructive and inappropriate, but there is the very real danger that other group members will become alienated and disenchanted enough to drop out of a group containing a chronic depressive talker.

The instructor found that a useful technique for dealing with C.C.'s depressive talk was to "reframe" C.C.'s negative statements in a more positive light. A difficult situation can often be reframed as an opportunity to practice new skills; negative input from others can be reframed as an opportunity to be assertive and see how it works. A tense day at work can be viewed as an opportunity to practice on-the-spot relaxation skills; a negative thought can be a chance to become aware of the thought process and substitute a more positive or constructive thought. In this way, depressive talkers provide the instructor with a challenge to model the skill of "positive reframing" and demonstrate to the group members that it is possible to look at the "flip side" of a negative thought or outlook and discover a constructive alternative.

In the case of C.C., the strategy of positive reframing was modeled regularly by the instructor. Other group members soon picked up on it and began employing it appropriately. Eventually, C.C. began to view negative events as "opportunities" to use some of the skills he was learning.

Monopolizers with Additional Problems

> "If only my life weren't such a disaster—my husband won't give me the time of day, and my children are only nice to me when they want something. How can I possibly feel better when I have nothing to look forward to?"

Personal problems or unfortunate life circumstances such as poor health, marital problems, parenting problems, a difficult job, or insufficient income can all be construed as insurmountable barriers to overcoming depression. A person who views life in this way is likely to return repeatedly to personal problems and to resist attempts at practical or step-by-step solutions. In addition, participants in the Coping with Depression course are often seeking psychological help for the first time, and they may hope for the resolution of problems that are beyond the scope of the class. Although participants may work on many problematic areas of their lives during class sessions, the course is not a cure-all, and some problems are better handled within a more traditional therapy situation.

> D.D. is a 59-year-old diabetic woman who is overweight and has an unhappy marriage. She frequently dwells upon her health concerns, voicing her conviction that the class will not be able to help her because her problems are serious, complex, and unsolvable.

In the case of D.D., her negative thoughts about her ability to learn to control her mood were the main problem. By reframing her unique difficulties as particularly challenging opportunities to apply the skills learned in the class, the instructor was able to assist D.D. in maintaining enthusiasm for the new material and ideas. D.D. was remarkably successful in gradually taking control of her life. By the end of the course, she had lost 20 pounds, had developed a daily habit of exercising, and had begun to enjoy and even look forward to the sessions. She had arranged with her physician to be fitted with a special pair of shoes that allowed her to walk more easily and thus get outdoor exercise; and finally, she reported that her relationship with her husband was vastly improved due to her change in attitude.

Some participants, of course, will have personal problems that are not so easily handled within the framework of the Coping with Depression course. When this situation occurs, the instructor may want to arrange a conference with the participant to discuss appropriate resources for working on problems that are outside the scope of the course. Acknowledging the participant's problems and making an appropriate referral should result in a substantial decrease in the participant's tendency to monopolize discussions with that issue.

Nonparticipators

At the other end of the spectrum are participants who are withdrawn or underinvolved in group discussions for some reason. The challenge for the instructor in this case is to draw the participant out and build upon his or her particular strengths to encourage class participation.

The Unmotivated Participant

"I have a confession to make. I haven't done my homework. And by the way, I won't be coming to class next week because I have another meeting I have to go to."

This participant appears to have a low level of motivation, has invested little time and energy in the course, and has poor rapport with the other participants and the instructor. Shyness in a group setting, a high level of performance anxiety, and low expectations about the effectiveness of the course may contribute to this problem. It is important for the group instructor to assess carefully the specific reason for the lack of participation.

E.E. is a 50-year-old recently divorced accountant who is living with his three grown children. The break-up of his twenty-year marriage precipitated a major depressive episode that resulted in his first psychiatric hospitalization. E.E. began the Coping with Depression course shortly after being discharged from the hospital. During early sessions, E.E. often sat gazing at the floor and refrained from talking unless he was asked a direct question. He did little, if any, of the homework and missed one session so he could "move to his new apartment." In addition to being depressed, E.E. was highly anxious and had abused Valium during the break-up of his marriage to reduce his anxiety.

In this situation, the participant is not able to benefit from the course because anxiety is interfering with learning new material. If this problem is not corrected early in the course, the participant may begin to feel increasingly like an outsider and may quietly withdraw from the class. Several strategies have proven successful with this kind of participant: a) using small group activities which are less threatening; b) engaging the participants in cohesiveness-building exercises early in the course; c) reminding the participant that he or she is an integral part of the group; d) making sure that selective reinforcement is used by the instructor and the other participants *whenever* the "nonparticipating participant" contributes to the class discussion; e) checking whether or not the participant understands and actually starts the *next* homework assignment with the rest of the group before the session ends; and f) encouraging the participant to do his or her homework by pointing out that it is not essential to do a perfect job on the homework assignments.

All of these strategies were employed with E.E. in the hope that he would increase his participation level and feel more like a part of the group. E.E. gradually began to interact more with the other participants during activities involving small groups of two or three participants. He took great pleasure in the "positive thought" exercise during which participants pointed out each other's positive qualities. After a few sessions, he indicated that he felt appreciated and closer to his classmates. When E.E. missed session six, several other participants offered to call him and let him know he was missed. The instructor also called him and asked him not to skip class simply because he hadn't done a "perfect job" on the homework and assured him that by coming to class he was doing something positive about his depression. E.E. never again missed a session. While E.E.'s homework compliance was never very high, it increased when he started new assignments with the rest of the class at the end of each session. It was as if getting a "foot in the door" increased the probability that E.E. would accomplish more of the assignment during the week.

The Slow Learner
"I don't understand how to do the homework assignment."

This participant has a difficult time learning new concepts and implementing new skills. The participant may seem motivated to improve his or her mood but often does not grasp the details of the homework assign-

123

ments. This may be a result of a low level of education, a low level of intelligence, anxiety interference, or poor concentration.

F.F. is a 46-year-old Mexican-American who is proud and very religious. F.F. left his wife and four children in Texas in order to take a job with an automobile factory in California. He has a history of several major depressive episodes, and the move away from his family precipitated another one. Having only an eighth-grade education, F.F. has some difficulty understanding the lecture material and completing the homework assignments. While the rest of the group members (many of whom have some college education) are capable of understanding the material with minimal explanation, F.F. needs more assistance.

In this situation, a well-motivated participant is learning more slowly than his classmates because of a poor educational background. The participant will eventually feel discouraged and left behind if this problem is not addressed early in the course. Several strategies may be employed with this kind of participant: a) individual attention and encouragement from the instructor during the break and after class to help the participant understand the assignments; b) encouragement and group support for the participant's accomplishments (however small) with regard to the homework; c) noting that everyone progresses at a different rate and that slow, gradual progress may help the participant to continue to improve his mood after the course has ended; d) encouraging the participant to call the instructor between sessions or arrange for the instructor to call the participant; e) implementing a "buddy system" for participants to call each other during the week to assist each other on the assignments; f) having participants begin the new assignments in class to make sure that everyone understands the assignment; and g) using as many visual aids as possible.

Many of these specific strategies were used on F.F. with excellent results. The group seemed to notice spontaneously that F.F. was a slow learner and began, with the instructor's encouragement, to point out evidence of progress (e.g., they noted that F.F. was smiling more, was more sociable, etc.). The instructor made a special effort to seek out F.F. during the breaks and after class in order to offer further assistance. F.F. was encouraged to call the instructor between sessions when he needed help with his homework assignments. It was pointed out during the pep talks that some people progress slower than others and that slow, gradual progress may actually help sustain motivation over a longer period of time. At the end of each session, the group instructor allotted at least 15 minutes for the participants to begin the new assignment. The instructor walked around the room checking each participant's progress, paying particular attention to F.F.'s needs without being obvious. F.F. began to improve steadily after the fifth and sixth sessions. He reported that people at his job began to make positive comments to him about his friendliness and good spirits.

The Nonresponder

> "This course is not working. I feel like I'm wasting my time and your time."

Approximately 15-20% of the participants in the Coping with Depression course do not improve following treatment and can be considered nonresponders. Nonresponders become discouraged after five or six sessions because most of the other participants are clearly improving while they are not. The nonresponder's lack of progress may be due to a number of factors: a) low motivation; b) low expectations regarding improvement; c) a poor match between the participant's problems and the specific skills taught in the course; d) an excess of stressful and aversive events in the participant's life; or e) any of the many special problems delineated in this chapter.

> G.G. is a 40-year-old school teacher and single mother living with three young children. She teaches ninth grade English and is very dissatisfied with her job. She is particularly irritated by the behavior problems of some of her students. She would prefer to be a writer or a higher level teacher. She has been depressed for a year and feels, after six sessions, that she has not improved at all. In fact, she feels increasingly overwhelmed with her work responsibilities and their interference with her family and social relationships.

This is an example of a situation in which a participant has continual aversive stimulation. She doesn't particularly like teaching uninterested ninth graders and is frustrated by trying to manage an overcrowded classroom. Her efforts to focus on relaxing, increasing pleasant activities, and thinking more constructively while at work had little impact. Strategies for dealing with this kind of problem include: a) attempt to remove the aversive stimuli; b) attempt to reduce the aversiveness of the stimuli; c) attempt to teach the participant coping strategies that change his or her perception of the stimuli; and d) point out that even though the skills offered in the course were not effective in improving the immediate situation, they may help to reduce the intensity or prevent future depressive episodes during a time when there are fewer negative events.

In G.G.'s case, several of the above tactics were utilized. She was given assignments to practice her relaxation exercises at work, to plan pleasant activities during her breaks, and to consult with other teachers to find out how they coped with their students. These strategies had little impact on her mood because she still found her job aversive. She was then given an assignment to develop a self-change plan aimed at finding a new and more satisfying job. This involved a step-by-step plan for looking for work (e.g., making phone calls, reading want ads, filling out applications, and going to interviews) and setting up a system for rewarding herself for her efforts. In addition, she was told that continuing in the course would provide her with an opportunity to learn new skills which would help her control her mood once she had improved her job situation. G.G. was provided with support and reinforcement for these activities by the group.

As it turned out, it was not until three months after the course was over that G.G. noticed improvement in her mood. Her self-change plan was a success in that she was hired by a community college to teach creative writing. The job was closer to home (thus requiring less commuting), and she thoroughly enjoyed teaching older students who were more motivated. She had more time to do some of the things she enjoyed, such as her own writing. At six-month follow-up, G.G. was no longer depressed.

The Sophisticated Participant

"I know how to do all of this already. I'm a therapist myself, and I use these techniques with my clients all the time. In fact, I've tried it all on myself before. Sometimes it works, sometimes it doesn't."

This participant feels that he or she knows all there is to know about treating depression. However, if this were true he or she probably would not be in the position of seeking help for severe depression. This pattern may be evident when the participant actually does know a lot but has not systematically applied this knowledge to him- or herself.

H.H. is a 30-year-old army veteran with multiple medical problems including paraplegia resulting from shrapnel wounds in Vietnam. He currently lives with his wife and their two children. He works full time as a counselor in his local community mental health center, making use of his M.A. degree in Counseling Psychology. H.H. has been doing therapy for over five years and is quite bright and experienced. He has never sought psychological help prior to enrolling in the course. While he has heard good reports about the course from some of his former clients, he is skeptical that the course will be able to help him.

126

In this situation, it was clear prior to the first session that the participant was very knowledgeable about therapy and psychological interventions for depression. The early recognition and acknowledgment of this fact allowed the instructor to anticipate several problems: a) H.H. may try to compete with the instructor in order to demonstrate his level of knowledge; b) H.H. may not do a thorough job on the homework assignments because he feels he's tried these techniques before; and c) the other participants may resent this participant's "know-it-all" attitude.

The instructor might try to deal with this situation by acknowledging in the initial interview that much of the material in the course is likely to be familiar to the participant because of his or her background in the area. The course can be described as an opportunity to try out some of the techniques in a more systematic and structured manner. The instructor might enlist the participant's "help" in providing suggestions and serving as a model for the other participants. This approach may gradually reduce the participant's resistance in a constructive way.

In the case of H.H., the above strategies were successfully employed. During the initial interview (prior to the first session of the course) H.H. was told that he obviously knew a lot about psychology and how to help other people. The instructor indicated that H.H. would be a welcome member of the group for these reasons. It was also tactfully pointed out that his prior attempts at helping himself had not been very effective and that the course could provide a more systematic approach to implementing some of the knowledge that he already had. H.H. became a model participant in that he did a thorough job on homework assignments and contributed freely to group discussions. H.H. used the group to explore his own feelings and took feedback graciously from the other participants. His presence was an asset rather than a liability. He became significantly more skilled at expressing his feelings and increasing his pleasant activity level. As a result, his mood improved dramatically.

Chapter 8

Assessment of Depression

The Coping with Depression course makes extensive use of assessment devices to diagnose the disorder and evaluate the factors that are contributing to it. Assessment is also the basis for determining the effectiveness of the course as a treatment for depression. Even though issues relating to assessment and diagnosis were introduced in Chapter 5, this chapter has been included to provide instructors with an overview of these topics.

Because of the heterogeneity of depressed individuals and the broad range of symptoms that they exhibit, it is important to establish explicit criteria and to identify specific behavior patterns that distinguish depression from other disorders. This is the goal of differential diagnosis—to use operational and nontheoretical tools to isolate depression as a unique disorder. The assessment devices relating to functional diagnosis will also be discussed as they are particularly relevant to the social learning approach to depression. Here, the goal is to pinpoint person-environment interactions that are contributing to depression. Because the skills that are taught in the Coping with Depression course are designed to bring about changes in functional events, these assessment procedures are an integral part of the treatment process.

Differential Diagnosis

There are four methods of assessment that can be used for differential diagnosis: 1) diagnostic systems; 2) symptom ratings; 3) self-report depression scales; and 4) observations of overt behavior. Although there are substantial differences between these approaches to diagnosis, they are complementary and should be used together to help the clinician to correctly identify depression as the presenting disorder.

Diagnostic Systems

The two diagnostic systems used most widely by clinicians and researchers are the DSM-III (Diagnostic and Statistical Manual of Mental Disorders, 3rd edition; American Psychiatric Association, 1980), and the RDC (Research Diagnostic Criteria; Spitzer, Endicott, and Robins, 1978). It has been demonstrated that these systems have good inter-rater reliability, especially when used with a semistructured interview schedule such as the SADS (Schedule for Affective Disorders and Schizophrenia; Endicott and Spitzer, 1978). In addition to syndrome description and criteria for major depression, the DSM-III includes criteria for dysthymic disorder, while the RDC includes criteria for minor and intermittent depressive disorders. Both systems also make a distinction between unipolar and bipolar depression—a distinction which is important for therapy outcome. There is evidence that bipolar depression is more amenable to psychopharmacological intervention, due to possible biochemical bases (Frazer, 1977), while unipolar depression is suggested to be more responsive to psychosocial interventions such as group treatment programs (McLean and Hakstian, 1979; Steinbrueck, Maxwell, & Howard, 1983).

Symptom Ratings

Factor-analytic studies have yielded evidence that depressed individuals exhibit symptoms which represent specific clusters of the depressive syndrome (e.g., Grinker et al., 1961). There are six such clusters: dysphoria, reduced rates of behavior, social-interactional problems, guilt, material burden, and somatic symptoms. These symptom clusters were described in Chapter 1 of this text. Each individual will exhibit a different combination of these symptom clusters; however, dysphoria is generally the one invariant symptom, expressed as feeling "empty," "blue," or "hopeless." Both the Feelings and Concerns Checklist by Grinker et al. and the Hamilton Psychiatric Rating Scale for Depression (Hamilton, 1960) have been shown to differentiate significantly between depressed and nondepressed patients, particularly when used in conjunction with the SADS interview.

Self-Report Depression Scales

Although self-report measures tend to be reactive to a certain degree, it has been shown that these measures correlate highly with each other, and that they differentiate depressed from nondepressed individuals (Lewinsohn and Teri, 1982). The scales used by the Coping with Depression program are the BDI (Beck Depression Inventory; Beck, Ward, Mendelson, Mock, and Erbaugh, 1961), and a visual analogue scale for the monitoring of daily mood (Lewinsohn, Muñoz, Youngren, and Zeiss, 1978). Other well-known self-report measures include the MMPI D scale, the SDS (Self-Rating Depression Scale; Zung, 1965), and the DACL (Depression Adjective Checklist; Lubin, 1965).

Observations of Overt Behavior

Depresssion as a syndrome includes a number of specific observable behaviors for which researchers have developed highly reliable coding systems (e.g., Reisinger, 1972; Robinson and Lewinsohn, 1973; Lewinsohn, 1976). The Ward Behavior Checklist for hospitalized patients (which includes behaviors such as talking, smiling, and taking a shower) correlates significantly with the Hamilton Psychiatric Rating Scale for Depression and the BDI.

Functional Diagnosis

As mentioned earlier, functional diagnosis is concerned with identifying the person-environment interactions that are contributing to depression. The goal of assessment is to pinpoint specific events and behavior patterns that are functionally related to depression. The types of events that are hypothesized to be related to depression are, of course, heavily influenced by the theoretical approach that is applied as a filter for focusing on salient events. Social learning theory suggests that depression occurs when an individual experiences a low rate of positive events and a high rate of unpleasant or punishing events. As a result, the assessment procedures described here are directed toward measuring rates of occurrence for these types of events. On the basis of functional diagnosis, it is possible to formulate an individualized plan for therapeutic intervention that is designed to bring about changes in these areas.

The PES (Pleasant Events Schedule; MacPhillamy and Lewinsohn, 1982) is a self-report instrument that provides specific data on the occurrence of common pleasurable activities and the enjoyment derived from them. Empirical research has shown that depressed individuals engage in fewer pleasant activities and that engagement in pleasant activities and mood level are substantially intercorrelated (Lewinsohn and Graf, 1973). Hence, the monitoring of pleasant events should be an integral part of treatment. The PES has been shown to have a high degree of correspondence between peer, observer, and self-ratings, and thus has been proven to be accurate and useful in the assessment of reinforcing events (MacPhillamy and Lewinsohn, 1982).

The PES Score Summary Sheet can be used by the clinician to identify a client's areas of potentially enjoyable activities, as well as the norms for his or her sex and age group. By focusing on the activities that are the most powerful for alleviating depression, the client can achieve the most dramatic gains in improving his or her mood. Further, having depressed individuals graph the number of pleasant events in relation to their daily mood levels can dramatically facilitate their understanding that enjoyable activities do have a direct impact on how they feel. This is an important motivator in behavior change. Since people differ markedly with regard to the specific kinds of activities they experience as pleasant, the PES can be used by both the clinician and the client to pinpoint specific pleasant activities to be increased.

It has been shown that depressed people also have a higher rate of occurrence of unpleasant events and experience them as more aversive than nondepressed persons (Lewinsohn and Talkington, 1979). Thus, the Unpleasant Events Schedule (UES) was developed, and has been found to differentiate between depressed and nondepressed persons (Lewinsohn, Mermelstein, Alexander, and MacPhillamy, 1984). There is a short 53-item version of the UES, as well as the 320-item schedule.

The Interpersonal Events Schedule (IES) consists of a list of 160 items, all of which involve interpersonal activities or cognitions concerning such interactions. Since depressed persons as a group tend to exhibit social-interactional problems, this scale can be used by the clinician to identify problematic interpersonal behaviors and events that are uniquely associated with depression, such as low rates of engagement and comfort in social activities, discomfort in being assertive, and negative cognitions concerning personal interactions (Youngren and Lewinsohn, 1980).

Conclusion

The clinical assessment of depressed individuals is a dual process involving differential and functional diagnosis. The assessment procedures that are used for differential diagnosis are aimed at establishing the level of depression in order to distinguish depressed individuals from nondepressed. Functional diagnosis is aimed at the identification of specific targets for therapeutic intervention and the evaluation of the effects of treatment on targeted events and behaviors. When used together, differential and functional diagnosis and the assessment procedures that they employ are an essential component of the Coping with Depression course.

Chapter 9

Research Findings

This chapter summarizes the results of several treatment outcome studies conducted at the University of Oregon Depression Research Unit (Brown & Lewinsohn, 1984b; Antonuccio, Lewinsohn, & Steinmetz, 1982; Steinmetz, Lewinsohn, & Antonuccio, 1983; Teri & Lewinsohn, 1982). The research was designed to address four questions: 1) Is the Coping with Depression course therapeutically effective? 2) Does the amount of instructor contact and the format in which the treatment is offered (group vs. individual) affect course outcome? 3) Are there consistent differences between instructors in the amount of improvement achieved with their students? If so, can these differences be predicted from pre-course instructor characteristics and from in-course instructor behavior? 4) Can improvement be predicted from pre-course participant characteristics?

Common Design Features

Course Content

The Coping with Depression course format was standardized across all studies and an instructor's manual (Steinmetz et al., 1979) was developed. Participants were required to complete reading assignments from the text and were given a participant workbook (an earlier version of Brown &

Lewinsohn, 1984a) containing goal statements, specific assignments for each unit, and monitoring forms for recording specific behaviors, thoughts, and feelings. The course consisted of 12 sessions scheduled over eight weeks. Sessions were held twice each week during the first four weeks, and once each week during the second four weeks. In addition, "class reunions" were scheduled one month and six months after the course had ended.

The first two sessions of the course were devoted to introducing participants to the class format and ground rules, explaining the social-learning approach to depression, and providing instruction in basic self-change skills (i.e., pinpointing, baselining, developing and implementing a self-change plan, and evaluating progress). The next eight sessions covered four specific skill areas: 1) learning how to relax; 2) increasing pleasant activities; 3) controlling thoughts; and 4) improving social skills and increasing positive social interactions. Two sessions were devoted to each skill area. During these sessions, participants were taught how to use each of the skills and they were provided with structured exercises designed to facilitate the acquisition of these skills. The last two sessions were devoted to creating a "Life Plan" in which participants identified the skills that they had found to be the most useful for preventing episodes of depression. All techniques were presented as skills to be learned and practiced. The syllabus for the course is shown in Table 9.1.

Table 9.1
Coping with Depression Course Syllabus

1. Depression and Social Learning
2. Self-Change Methods
3. Relaxation and Depression
4. Relaxation in Everyday Situations
5. Pleasant Activities and Depression
6. Formulating a Pleasant Activities Plan
7. Thinking and Depression
8. Formulating a Plan for Constructive Thinking
9. Social Skills: The Ability To Be Assertive
10. Using Your Social Skills
11. Maintaining Your Gains
12. Developing a Life Plan

The course was designed to be offered within a "class modality." All classes, including the follow-up sessions at one month and six months, met for two hours. Class time was divided between *lectures* intended to supplement course readings, and reviewing homework assignments (which included self-monitoring and practicing the various skills presented in the course). Typically, participants were asked to share with the class their experiences in doing the homework (sometimes the class was divided into smaller groups to facilitate the interaction of participants). When appropriate, instructors modeled and participants role-played responses to particular problem situations while other participants were encouraged to provide constructive feedback.

Participants

Participants were recruited through community-wide announcements similar to those described in Chapter 4. Letters and fliers were mailed to mental health professionals and community agencies. Advertisements and public service announcements were also arranged with various media.

Descriptive characteristics of the participants in each of the studies are summarized in Table 9.2. Consistent with the educational philosophy of the course, exclusion criteria were minimal. Individuals were excluded if they showed evidence of mental retardation, dyslexia, serious visual or auditory impairment, bipolar disorder, schizophrenia or schizoaffective disorder, or acute substance abuse. Participants who were already receiving psychotherapy, counseling, or pharmacotherapy for depression or other problems were not excluded from the program.

Course Format

Subjects receiving treatment via the Coping with Depression course (class modality) were compared with subjects in the following conditions.

Waiting list control group. In the study by Brown and Lewinsohn (1984b), one-fourth of the participants were randomly assigned to a delayed treatment condition. For an eight-week period corresponding to the duration of the course for participants in the immediate treatment conditions, the waiting list participants received no treatment. At the end of this eight-week period, all of the subjects in the waiting list control group were then enrolled in the Coping with Depression course.

Individual tutoring. In this condition, the course was taught on a one-to-one basis. Individual tutoring sessions were intended to last 50 minutes or less; the average length of sessions was 49.0 minutes (range = 25 to 75 minutes). As in the class condition, individual tutoring sessions were primarily devoted to presenting information that supplemented course readings and reviewing homework assignments. When appropriate, instructors modeled and participants role-played responses to particular problem situations.

Phone contact modality. In this condition, instructors met with participants and the entire course was previewed during the first session. The rationale for the course and an overview for each unit were provided; assignments and the various monitoring forms were briefly explained. All subsequent sessions were conducted via telephone contacts which were initiated by the instructors at regularly scheduled times. Phone contacts were designed to provide participants with encouragement and assistance in com-

Table 9.2

	Brown & Lewinsohn, 1984b	Steinmetz, Lewinsohn & Antonuccio, 1983 Antonuccio, Lewinsohn & Steinmetz, 1982	Teri & Lewinsohn, 1982
N	75	112	84
% Female	73	69	62
% Diagnosed Depressed at Start of Treatment	81	67	71
Age: Mean	37	36	33
Age: Range	19-74	22-59	20-60
Age: Standard Deviation	11.5	10.6	13.9
% Graduate Training	30	13	10
% Completed College	15	19	32
% Attended Some College	38	46	39
% High School Graduate	13	17	18
% Attended Some High School	4	5	1
% Married	45	53	46
% Separated, Divorced, Widowed	35	31	29
% Single	20	16	25

pleting course assignments. During each phone contact, instructors attempted to improve the participant's general mood level, reviewed the participant's homework assignments, and provided assistance in dealing with problems in comprehending and/or completing course assignments. The instructors then briefly previewed the next session including a statement of goals and the homework assignment. Phone contacts were intended to last 15 minutes, but actually lasted an average of 18.4 minutes (range = 10 to 35 minutes).

Individual behavior therapy. In the study by Teri and Lewinsohn (1982), the class condition was compared with individual behavior therapy. The latter was based on a treatment called "Decrease Unpleasant Events and Increase Pleasant Activities" (Lewinsohn, Sullivan, & Grosscup, 1980). Table 9.3 summarizes the components of this treatment.

Table 9.3
Outline of "Decrease Unpleasant Events and Increase Pleasant Activities" Treatment Module
(Lewinsohn, Sullivan, & Grosscup, 1980)

I. Diagnostic Assessment plus 12 Treatment Sessions
II. Functional Assessment
    A. Unpleasant Events Schedule
    B. Pleasant Events Schedule
    C. Activity Schedule (80 Pleasant and 80 Unpleasant)
    D. Mood Ratings
    E. Plot Daily Mood and Activities
III. Tactics
    A. Rationale Presentation
    B. Pinpointing Key Pleasant and Unpleasant Events
    C. Daily Monitoring to Set Goals and Evaluate Progress
    D. Teach Skills to Change Problematic Patterns of Interaction
        1. Relaxation
        2. Time Management and Daily Planning
        3. Assertiveness
        4. Cognitive Tactics
    E. Maintenance and Prevention

The focus of this treatment was to change the quality and the quantity of the depressed patient's interactions by increasing positive events and decreasing negative events. It was time limited (12 sessions), highly structured, and a therapist manual was written to standardize the procedures. The treatment made extensive use of the PES (Pleasant Events Schedule; MacPhillamy & Lewinsohn, 1971) and the UES (Unpleasant Events Schedule; Lewinsohn, 1975) to pinpoint specific person-environment interactions that were related to the patient's depression. An activity schedule (Lewinsohn, 1976) consisting of 80 items rated by the patients as most pleasant and frequent, and 80 items rated by the patients as most unpleasant and frequent, was constructed and patients began to monitor the occurrence of pleasant and unpleasant activities and their mood. They continued this daily monitoring for the duration of the treatment. The covariation of certain pleasant and unpleasant events with changes in mood was used to pinpoint the specific person-environment interactions that were contributing to the patient's dysphoria. The focus of treatment was to decrease the frequency and the subjective aversiveness of unpleasant events while achieving corresponding increases in positive events.

The general goal of the treatment was to teach depressed persons skills they could use to change problematic patterns of interaction with the environment and skills for maintaining these changes after the termination of therapy. To accomplish the goals of treatment, therapists used a wide range of cognitive-behavioral interventions such as assertiveness training, relaxation methods, time management techniques, and cognitive procedures intended to allow the person to deal more adaptively with aversive situations. A more detailed description of this approach is presented in the study by Lewinsohn, Sullivan, and Grosscup, 1980.

Assessment Procedures

Each study assessed different variables depending upon the specific hypotheses under investigation. A core assessment battery, however, was constant across studies. Self-report measures of depression included the BDI (Beck Depression Inventory; Beck, Ward, Mendelson, Mock, & Erbaugh, 1961) and the CES-D (Center for Epidemiological Studies—Depression scale; Radloff, 1977). The BDI consists of 21 items that list symptoms classified by the degree of severity and duration for each symptom. The CES-D is a 20-item self-report measure; items are rated on a scale of 0-3 that corresponds to the degree of severity and frequency of occurrence for the previous week. Diagnoses of depression and other psychopathological syndromes were obtained by utilizing the decision rules specified by the RDC (Research Diagnostic Criteria; Spitzer, Endicott, & Robins, 1978). Information was gathered from participants using a two-hour semi-structured, pretreatment interview, the SADS (Schedule for Affective Disorders and Schizophrenia; Endicott & Spitzer, 1978). For each episode of disturbance the interviewer recorded the diagnosis, age at onset, and duration of the episode. In addition, a second and much shorter version of the interview, the SADS-C (Schedule for Affective Disorders and Schizophrenia—Change version; Endicott & Spitzer, 1978) was used to measure change from pretreatment to post-treatment and follow-up.

Interviewers

The diagnostic interviewers were a carefully selected group of graduate and advanced undergraduate students who had been trained in SADS and RDC procedures. All interviewers had taken a year-long seminar in "Diagnostic Interviewing" in which intensive didactic and experiential training in the use of the SADS and RDC procedures had been provided. The kappa statistic (Cohen, 1960), which measures how well two raters agree beyond the level predicted by chance, was used to measure inter-rater reliability. For the four main diagnostic categories in each study, kappas were comparable to those reported by Endicott and Spitzer (1978).

Instructors and Therapists

The course instructors were advanced graduate students in Clinical and Counseling Psychology. All course instructors and therapists were required to complete a specialized three-month training program before conducting the Coping with Depression course or individual behavior therapy. They also participated in weekly group supervision during each study. Instructors and therapists were expected to follow their respective treatment protocols as closely as possible.

Findings

Outcome—Course Efficacy

Whether or not the course is therapeutically effective is not an easy question to answer unequivocally. Under ideal circumstances, it would be extremely useful to compare the treatment group with a no-treatment control group; but ethically it is very difficult not to offer treatment to people who are depressed and potentially suicidal. Our solution to this problem was to randomly assign a group of the individuals in the first study (Brown & Lewinsohn, 1984b) to a delayed treatment condition. This group received treatment after an eight-week waiting period; during this time they were encouraged to call the course instructor if they needed help. For the first eight weeks, then, these subjects received very little in the way of "treatment."

The results in Table 9.4 indicate that the subjects in this first study who received active treatment showed more clinical improvement than the subjects in the delayed treatment condition. The results also suggest that the improvement demonstrated by participants in the Coping with Depression course was substantial at post-treatment, and that these gains were maintained at one-month and six-month follow-up. Our own studies, and studies by other researchers, suggest that the degree of improvement realized by participants in the Coping with Depression course is comparable to that of patients in individual therapy (e.g., Bellack, Hersen, & Himmelhoch, 1981; Rush & Beck, 1978; McLean & Hakstian, 1979). Recognizing the usual limitations concerning generalizing and the need for cross-

Table 9.4

Beck Depression Inventory Scores from Three Treatment Outcome Studies Involving the Coping with Depression Course

Study	RX Condition(s)	Pre-RX $\overline{X}$	Pre-RX S.D.	Post-RX $\overline{X}$	Post-RX S.D.	Follow-Up 1 Month $\overline{X}$	Follow-Up 1 Month S.D.	Follow-Up 6 Month $\overline{X}$	Follow-Up 6 Month S.D.
Brown & Lewinsohn, 1984b	Class N = 31	19.8	7.7	7.6	7.0	6.6	6.2	6.4	6.9
	Individual N = 15	24.4	8.6	9.5	7.7	11.1	9.4	7.4	7.5
	Phone N = 12	20.1	7.5	10.8	7.2	10.0	9.2	9.5	6.2
	Delayed N = 13	20.5	9.6	13.9	8.7				
Steinmetz, Lewinsohn, & Antonuccio, 1983	Class N = 93	20.5	9.4	6.8	6.1	6.5	6.1	7.9	8.5
Teri & Lewinsohn, 1982	Class N = 55	19.9	11.0	4.7	5.1	5.8	6.0	5.3	7.2
	Individual N = 29	18.2	11.1	2.8	3.8	5.1	7.0	8.0	12.1

validation by other researchers, it appears that the Coping with Depression course is a viable and cost-effective treatment approach for depressed out-patients.

Comparison of Group, Individual, and Phone Contact Procedures

We have also investigated whether or not the amount of therapist contact and the format in which the course is offered have an effect on treatment outcome. In the study by Brown and Lewinsohn (1984b), three active treatments were compared (class, individual, and phone contact). In the study by Teri and Lewinsohn (1982), the class condition was compared with individual behavior therapy. The latter was based on the treatment protocol summarized in Table 9.2. The results in Table 9.4 indicate that differences between all of the active treatment conditions were small and statistically insignificant.

Therapist Variables Related to Outcome

The instructors for Coping with Depression courses have all been advanced doctoral students in Clinical and Counseling Psychology who, in addition to having extensive supervised experience in individual psychotherapy as part of their graduate training, have been carefully trained to conduct the course. The second study was designed by Antonuccio, Lewinsohn, and Steinmetz (1982) to identify the instructor variables that were related to treatment outcome. The assumption was that there would be systematic differences between instructors in the amount of improvement shown by their students and that these differences would be related to instructor variables. A repeated measurements design was used for the study. Eight course instructors conducted two consecutive treatment groups consisting of five to eight subjects per group. The instructors were then evaluated on a large number of variables including pretreatment instructor characteristics, instructor behavior and style during treatment, and group behavior and group processes. These instructor variables were hypothesized to be related to treatment outcome on the basis of a review of the literature. The major finding of this study was that even though the instructors differed significantly on many of the variables (e.g., group cohesiveness, group participation, instructor warmth, instructor enthusiasm, instructor expectations, on-task activities, and so on) the main effect in the ANOVA due to instructor differences was not statistically significant. That is, the instructors did not differ in how much improvement their respective students showed at the end of the course. Similar results were also obtained in a study by Brown and Lewinsohn (1984b). Since all of the groups showed substantial improvement from pretreatment to post-treatment, these results are an indication

143

that our instructor training procedures and criteria for instructor selection are quite adequate (i.e., they minimize any systematic effects that instructor characteristics might have on outcome and insure that instructors will be consistently successful).

Participant Variables Predictive of Outcome

While our results show that a majority of depressed individuals are improved at the end of treatment, it is also true that a significant proportion (approximately 20%) stay depressed. This figure is relatively constant across studies. Several studies have been conducted to determine if it is possible to predict which individuals will not respond to this type of treatment. All of these studies have included overlapping participant variables with the goal of identifying and cross-validating any positive findings.

Prior to summarizing the findings relating to participant characteristics that are predictive of improvement, it should be emphasized that our dependent variable so far has been post-course depression level. Post-course depression level has been established independently of pre-course depression level by using analysis of covariance, computing residual gains scores, or by entering pre-course depression level as the first variable into the multiple regression. We have used these particular analyses because our initial interest

Table 9.5
Pretreatment Variables
which Predict Improvement in
Coping with Depression Course Participants

	Approximate Correlations
1. Pretreatment Depression Level (BDI)	− .45
2. Expected Improvement (EBDI)	.34
3. Satisfaction with Major Life Roles	.30
4. Concurrent Treatment	− .25
5. Perceived Social Support from Family	.20
6. Physical Handicap, Disabling Disease, Recent Surgery	− .25
7. Suicidal Behavior	− .40
8. Perceived Control	.20

Correlations 2 through 8 are partial correlations with post-BDI after controlling for pre-BDI. Multiple correlations with post-BDI have been approximately .75, accounting for approximately 56% of the variance.

was to identify the distinguishing characteristics of participants who show the greatest amount of change (improvement) from pretreatment to post-treatment.

The results from our first two studies (Brown & Lewinsohn, 1984b; Steinmetz, Lewinsohn, & Antonuccio, 1983) are summarized in Table 9.5. As might be expected, the most powerful predictor of post-course depression level is pretreatment depression level as measured by the BDI. Those who are the most depressed at the beginning of the course are still the most depressed at the end of treatment. This result supports Garfield's (1978) statement that pretreatment severity should always be taken into account in the prediction of treatment outcome because the correlation between pretreatment and post-treatment scores is typically positive and substantial.

As shown in Table 9.5, seven variables accounted for outcome variance beyond that explained by pretreatment BDI scores:

1. **Expected improvement.** This was measured by asking participants to complete, at intake, the BDI according to how they predict they will feel at the end of the course. Participants who expected to be the most symptom free at the end of treatment actually were the most improved.

2. **Satisfaction with major life roles.** Participants who had expressed more satisfaction (using a seven-point scale) with 18 life areas generally considered to be important were also the most improved.

3. **Concurrent treatment.** Participants who were *not* concurrently receiving additional treatment for depression (psychotherapy and/or antidepressant medications) were more improved.

4. **Perceived social support from family members.** Better treatment outcome was obtained by individuals with more perceived social support.

5. **Physical problems.** Patients who did not have a physical handicap, a disabling disease, or recent surgery were more improved.

6. **Suicidal attempts.** Those who had a history of a suicidal attempt were less improved.

7. **Perceived mastery.** This was assessed via participants' ratings of three items designed to reflect perceptions of control over one's life (e.g., "I have little control over things that happen to me"). Participants who felt that they had greater mastery were more improved.

The following pretreatment variables did *not* predict improvement in Coping with Depression course participants:

1. **Symptoms.** Endogeneity, number of previous episodes, previous alcohol and drug abuse.

2. **Demographics.** Sex, income, occupational level, and number of children. Age and marital status have yielded inconsistent findings. In at least

one of our studies being younger and being single were positively related to outcome.

3. Cognitions. Locus of control (I-E), irrational beliefs, acceptance of course rationale.

4. Stressful life events. As measured by the Holmes & Rahe scale (1967).

5. Other participant characteristics. Manageability, treatability, likeability (Wills, 1978), motivation (participants estimated the percentage of homework assignments they expected to complete as a measure of motivation), and social skill.

The following variables are currently being investigated:

1. Ability of the client to form a therapeutic relationship (Strupp & Hadley, 1979; Strupp, 1980).

2. Learned resourcefulness (Rosenbaum, 1980).

3. Interpersonal dependency (Hirschfeld et al., 1976).

4. Sex role (Bem, 1974).

5. Physical exercise.

6. Existence of problems with children.

7. Expressed emotionality (Vaughn & Leff, 1976).

Summary and Conclusions

Over the past five years we have used the Coping with Depression course with more than 300 depressed individuals. As a group, participants have realized substantial improvement pre- to post-treatment, and these changes have been maintained at one-month and six-month follow-up. We also interpret the results to indicate that our criteria for the selection of instructors and our instructor training procedures are quite adequate. Among a large number of participant variables that were hypothesized on a priori grounds to be predictive of positive outcome, only a few have emerged consistently. These need to be cross-validated. With hindsight, all of the variables shown in Table 9.5 are intuitively plausible except for the findings relating to concurrent treatment. The finding that concurrent treatment is a negative predictor of outcome is thought provoking, particularly since those participants were not more severely depressed initially. It is possible that concurrent involvement in a different form of treatment somehow interfered with participants' motivation or ability to actively work on learning and using the coping skills presented in the course.

Chapter 10

Future Directions

While it is easy to make enthusiastic statements about the Coping with Depression course (e.g., most participants are improved, these improvements are maintained at one-month and six-month follow-up, and the drop-out rate is quite low), it is equally easy to suggest directions for future research. The following issues seem to be the most urgent: 1) evaluating the long-term effects of the course; 2) delineating more carefully the characteristics of depressed individuals who do not respond to the course and who might respond to other treatments; and 3) designing and evaluating modifications of the Coping with Depression course for use with populations that are different from those that have been studied so far.

Long-Term Maintenance

There have been relatively few studies on the long-term effects of treatment for depression, but the results of a recent study by Keller and Shapiro (1981) suggest that the beneficial effects of treatment may fade with time for many patients. In a one-year follow-up of persons treated for depression, Keller and Shapiro (1981) found that only 30% were symptom free during the first year after treatment.

Even in the absence of precise follow-up data, it is safe to assume that at least some of the participants who are improved at the end of the Coping with Depression course will relapse (i.e., develop another episode of depression). Specifically, there are two questions that need to be addressed: 1) in absolute terms, how many of the former participants become depressed again; and 2) has participation in the course reduced the probability that they will become depressed in the future? Gonzales, Lewinsohn, Teri, and Clarke are currently conducting a long-term follow-up study in which all of the former participants in the Coping with Depression courses offered at the University of Oregon will be reassessed up to three years post-treatment. The results of this study will, hopefully, not only provide information on the two questions just mentioned, but may also suggest modifications in the course that would enhance long-term outcome. Pending the results of this study, modifications aimed at the generalization and maintenance of treatment gains might include additional therapeutically structured follow-up sessions, such as "booster" sessions or advanced workshops for former participants. Since the Coping with Depression course is a "basic" course designed to be something of a "smorgasbord" of coping skills, more advanced training in specific problem areas such as negative cognitions, assertiveness, time management, and relaxation would be a logical next step to encourage maintenance of treatment gains.

The Characteristics of Nonresponders

While our research on the Coping with Depression course clearly indicates that most of the participants improve significantly, approximately 20% fail to improve. The fact that this figure is consistent with research on failure rates for other treatments of depression (e.g., McLean & Hakstian, 1979; Weissman & Klerman, 1977; Weissman, Klerman, Prusoff, Sholomskas, & Padin, 1981) should not be taken as an excuse to ignore this very important subgroup of depressed individuals.

The recent literature includes a number of studies that have examined the patient characteristics hypothesized to be related to successful treatment outcome (Bisno, Thompson, Breckenridge, & Gallagher, 1982; Brown & Lewinsohn, 1984b; McLean & Hakstian, 1979; Rehm, 1981; Steinmetz, Lewinsohn, & Antonuccio, 1983; Weissman, Prusoff, & Klerman, 1978). Some promising results have already been obtained. However, it is clear that more research is needed to cross-validate these findings and to identify additional distinguishing characteristics of nonresponders.

The fact that regular attendance and favorable expectations regarding outcome are predictive of positive treatment response (Steinmetz, Lewinsohn, & Antonuccio, 1983) suggests that the Coping with Depression course might be modified to take advantage of these variables. The relationship between these participant variables and outcome might even be presented to participants as part of the introduction to the course in a direct attempt to encourage a positive expectancy and regular attendance.

The combined use of antidepressant medications (and perhaps other psychotherapeutic approaches) with the Coping with Depression course for some participants also deserves further exploration. The data that we have collected thus far suggest that the combination is counterproductive; however, this does not rule out the possibility that the correct criteria may not have been used to select the participants that would benefit from combining the course with the administering of drugs or psychotherapy.

Comparison of the Coping with Depression course with treatments that use antidepressant medications poses an especially important focus for future research. There is overwhelming evidence that pharmacotherapy is also successful in treating unipolar depression (Morris & Beck, 1974; Rush et al., 1977; Weissman et al., 1981). As a result, many depressives are being treated with antidepressant medicines. Because of the availability of these two rather distinct types of treatment, it is of considerable clinical importance to obtain a greater understanding of which persons benefit from which treatment. Future research might thus be directed not only at comparing these two types of treatment but also at identifying the factors that predict the response of a given individual to each type of treatment.

Modifications for Other Populations

The Coping with Depression course can and should be adapted for use with other populations. In addition to modifying the course for use with adolescents and the elderly, it might also be an effective adjunct to the treatment of alcoholics or medical patients. Turner, Wehl, Cannon, and Craig (1980) have already obtained encouraging results with the behavioral treatment of depression in alcoholics using techniques similar to those employed in the Coping with Depression course. It would also be of interest to discover whether the so-called "chronic" depressives (i.e., those individuals who have not responded to other treatments) will respond to the Coping with Depression course. At the Reno VA Medical Center, research is currently under way to determine the effectiveness of the Coping with Depression course with individuals who have not responded to antidepressant medications (Antonuccio, Akins, Chatham, Monagin, Tearnan, & Ziegler, 1984).

Other populations for which the efficacy of a modified version of the course should be evaluated might include patients with chronic and disabling physical illnesses such as heart disease, kidney disease, cancer, or chronic pain (i.e., diseases that require major changes in the person's life style and which are often accompanied by depression).

149

Since age was a variable that was associated with poor outcome in at least one of our studies (Steinmetz, Lewinsohn, & Antonuccio, 1983), modifications to suit the special needs of older individuals might also prove to be beneficial. Such modifications might focus on the special problems of the elderly (e.g., high rate of loss of friends and loved ones due to death, cognitive and physical problems). Thompson and his colleagues at the University of Southern California and at the Palo Alto VA Medical Center have evaluated the effectiveness of a Coping course specifically designed for depressed elders (Thompson, Gallagher, Nies, & Epstein, 1982). Thompson et al. have anecdotally noted a more vigorous interest among the elderly in a Coping course when it was offered with a more positive, preventative focus. In a pilot study (Teri, Mermelstein, & Finch, personal communication), a modified version of the Coping with Depression course was recently offered to the elderly at a senior center. Entitled "Enriching Your Later Life," the course was designed for individuals over 50 who were "interested in enhancing their lives, and improving their feelings about themselves." The goal of the course was to help participants learn how to combat feelings of sadness, loneliness, or the "blues" by working on various aspects of their lives that may have an impact on their mood (e.g., activities, social life, and physical health). A similar type of research is under way at the Palo Alto VA Medical Center (Steinmetz, Zeiss, & Thompson, 1983; Steinmetz, Thompson, Breckenridge, & Gallagher, 1984); "Increasing Life Satisfaction" courses are being offered at a number of senior centers and community agencies. Both treatment outcome and the process of change are being evaluated by this research group.

Another potential modification would involve offering the Coping course as a "Life Skills" course in high schools or adult education classes. It seems reasonable to assume that the skills taught in the course are appropriate for nondepressed as well as depressed individuals.

The Coping with Depression course has great potential for modification and evaluation with a wide variety of problems and populations. The actualization of this potential awaits further empirical and clinical investigation. We hope that by making this text available, other clinicians and researchers will be stimulated to explore new applications for this treatment format.

Appendices

Appendix 1.1
The Coping with Depression Course—Feedback

1) As a clinician, what do you find lacking in background and introductory material in this manual?

2) Which sessions do you find particularly problematic? Are there specific problems inherent in certain sessions, either in the material itself, or in presenting it?

3) What kinds of clients are the most problematic in which sessions (e.g., disruptive clients in the relaxation session)?

4) What methods would you suggest for dealing with these kinds of client-related problems?

5) Do you have suggestions for training clinicians to use the course in other settings?

6) How effective was the course in alleviating depression? If available, please note Beck Depression Inventory scores before and after treatment.

7) Additional comments or suggestions for general course improvement:

Please mail the completed form to:

The Coping with Depression Course
University of Oregon/Straub Hall
Department of Psychology
Human Neuropsychology Laboratory
Eugene, OR 97403

THANK YOU FOR YOUR HELP!

Appendix 4.1
Sample Letter

Dear Colleague:

Depression is one of the nation's most common mental health problems, affecting nearly twenty percent of all Americans at some time in their lives.

Individuals who have been (or are now) experiencing depression may wish to participate in the Psychology Clinic's eight-week Coping with Depression program. The first of the sessions begins January 12, 1981. Another series will be offered in the spring.

A fee of $100 or $150, depending on family income, will be charged for the eight-week course. Half of the fee can be earned back by completing questionnaires and participating in personal interviews.

We would appreciate your assistance in informing potential participants about this program. A flier is enclosed that you may wish to post in a convenient location.

Please call 686-4966 if you would like more information. We would be happy to answer any questions you might have.

Sincerely,

Appendix 4.2

Television and radio news release.   For immediate release.

UO Program Offers Help for Depression.

A program designed to help participants combat depression will be offered by the University of Oregon beginning January 12, 1981.

Sponsored by the UO Psychology Department, "Coping with Depression" is open to the public.

The eight-week program is based on the assumption that people can overcome depression by learning and using different skills.

Participants are helped to decide what they want to change about themselves and then set up a step-by-step plan to achieve it.

Skills include relaxation training, self-change techniques, constructive thinking, balancing positive and negative thoughts, planning pleasant activities, and using social skills effectively.

Program participants will work individually or in small groups.

The individual sessions involve a therapist who helps participants cope with specific problems.

Group sessions are structured as a course with a text (*Control Your Depression,* Lewinsohn et al., Prentice-Hall, 1986) and a workbook containing reading and homework assignments.

The fee for twelve sessions is $100 or $150, depending on family income. Half of the fee can be earned back by completing questionnaires and participating in personal interviews.

Interested persons may call 686-4966 for more information and to arrange for an interview.

Appendix 4.3
Sample Newspaper Ad

If you've
been depressed and
wondering when you'll get
over it, maybe it's time to talk to us.

We believe depression is a common
feeling caused by problems in living.
And that individuals can learn skills to help them cope
with their problems and overcome their depression.

Our Coping with Depression program involves eight
weeks of sessions with a trained therapist.

*Participants can learn how
to apply these useful skills:*
• RELAXATION • SCHEDULING • ASSERTIVENESS
• SELF-CHANGE • THOUGHT CONTROL
CALL THE
University of Oregon Psychology Department at
686-4966
and ask us about our program

DON'T PUT UP WITH FEELING DOWN

You can learn how to control your mood.

- Relax and ease anxiety
- Change old habits
- Think more constructively
- Control positive and negative thoughts
- Increase pleasant activities

You could learn how to overcome and prevent feelings of depression. If you have experienced problems with depression, you should know about some useful skills that could help you.

The University of Oregon Psychology Clinic is now offering a program for "Coping with Depression."

Participants set their own goals and work in a comfortable and supportive setting.

A fee based on family income will be charged.

CALL 686-4966
for information

157

Appendix 4.5

Dear Friend:

It has been several months since you completed your Coping with Depression Course.

We hope that what you learned has continued to be useful and you are feeling more in control of your mood. In fact, now might be a good time to take a look at your life plan and see how you are progressing toward your goal.

We also want to let you know we are continuing to offer our program in small groups as well as individualized sessions. This program will begin on January 12, 1981. A second series of sessions will be offered in the spring.

If you have friends or relatives to whom you would like to recommend our program, they can call us at 686-4966 to get more information or to set up an interview.

With best wishes,

Appendix 4.6

(from Ethical Principles of Psychologists,
Copyright 1981 by the American Psychological Association.
Reprinted by permission of the publisher and author.)

PUBLIC STATEMENTS

Public statements, announcements of services, advertising, and promotional activities of psychologists serve the purpose of helping the public make informed judgments and choices. Psychologists represent accurately and objectively their professional qualifications, affiliations, and functions, as well as those of the institutions or organizations with which they or the statements may be associated. In public statements providing psychological information or professional opinions or providing information about the availability of psychological products, publications, and services, psychologists base their statements on scientifically acceptable psychological findings and techniques with full recognition of the limits and uncertainties of such evidence.

a. When announcing or advertising professional services, psychologists may list the following information to describe the provider and services provided: name, highest relevant academic degree earned from a regionally accredited institution, date, type and level of certification or license, diplomate status, APA membership status, address, telephone number, office hours, a brief listing of the type of psychological services offered, an appropriate presentation of fee information, foreign languages spoken, and policy with regard to third-party payments. Additional relevant or important consumer information may be included if not prohibited by other sections of these Ethical Principles.

b. In announcing or advertising the availability of psychological products, publications, or services, psychologists do not present their affiliation with any organization in a manner that falsely implies sponsorship or certification by that organization. In particular and for example, psychologists do not state APA membership or fellow status in a way to suggest that such status implies specialized professional competence or qualifications. Public statements include, but are not limited to, communication by means of periodical, book, list, directory, television, radio, or motion picture. They do not contain: (1) a false, fraudulent, misleading, deceptive, or unfair statement; (2) a misinterpretation of fact or a statement likely to mislead or deceive because in context it makes only a partial disclosure of relevant facts; (3) a testimonial from a patient regarding the quality of a psychologist's services or products; (4) a statement intended or likely to create false or unjustified expectations of favorable results; (5) a statement implying unusual, unique, or one-of-a-kind abilities; (6) a statement concerning the comparative desirability of offered services; (7) a statement of direct solicitation of individual clients.

c. Psychologists do not compensate or give anything of value to a representative of the press, radio, television, or other communication medium in anticipation of or in return for professional publicity in a news item. A paid advertisement must be identified as such, unless it is apparent from the context that it is a paid advertisement. If communicated to the public by use of radio or television, an advertisement is prerecorded and approved for broadcast by the psychologist, and a recording of the actual transmission is retained by the psychologist.

d. Announcements or advertisements of "personal growth groups," clinics, and agencies give a clear statement of purpose and a clear description of the experiences to be provided. The education, training, and experience of the staff members are appropriately specified.

e. Psychologists associated with the development or promotion of psychological devices, books, or other products offered for commercial sale make reasonable efforts to ensure that announcements and advertisements are presented in a professional, scientifically acceptable, and factually informative manner.

f. Psychologists do not participate for personal gain in commercial announcements or advertisements recommending to the public the purchase or use of proprietary or single-source products or services when that participation is based solely upon their identification as psychologists.

g. Psychologists present the science of psychology and offer their services, products, and publications fairly and accurately, avoiding misrepresentation through sensationalism, exaggeration, or superficiality. Psychologists are guided by the primary obligation to aid the public in developing informed judgments, opinions, and choices.

h. As teachers, psychologists ensure that statements in catalogs and course outlines are accurate and not misleading, particularly in terms of subject matter to be covered, bases for evaluating progress, and the nature of course experiences. Announcements, brochures, or advertisements describing workshops, seminars, or other educational programs accurately describe the audience for which the program is intended as well as eligibility requirements, educational objectives, and nature of the materials to be covered. These announcements also accurately represent the education, training, and experience of the psychologists presenting the programs and any fees involved.

i. Public announcements or advertisements soliciting research participants in which clinical services or other professional services are offered as an inducement make clear the nature of the services as well as the costs and other obligations to be accepted by participants in the research.

j. A psychologist accepts the obligation to correct others who represent the psychologist's professional qualifications, or associations with products or services, in a manner incompatible with these guidelines.

k. Individual diagnostic and therapeutic services are provided only in the context of a professional psychological relationship. When personal advice is given by means of public lecture or demonstrations, newspapers, or magazine articles, radio or television programs, mail, or similar media, the psychologist utilizes the most current relevant data and exercises the highest level of professional judgment.

l. Products that are described or presented by means of public lectures or demonstrations, newspaper or magazine articles, radio or television programs, or similar media meet the same recognized standards as exist for products used in the context of a professional relationship.

WELFARE OF THE CONSUMER

Psychologists respect the integrity and protect the welfare of the people and groups with whom they work. When conflicts of interest arise between clients and psychologists' employing institutions, psychologists clarify the nature and direction of their loyalties and responsibilities and keep all parties informed of their commitments. Psychologists fully inform consumers as to the purpose and nature of an evaluative, treatment, educational, or training procedure, and they freely acknowledge that clients, students, or participants in research have freedom of choice with regard to participation.

a. Psychologists are continually cognizant of their own needs and of their potentially influential position vis-a-vis persons such as clients, students, and subordinates. They avoid exploiting the trust and dependency of such persons. Psychologists make every effort to avoid dual relationships that could impair their professional judgment or increase the risk of exploitation. Examples of such dual relationships include, but are not limited to, research with and treatment of employees, students, supervisees, close friends, or relatives. Sexual intimacies with clients are unethical.

b. When a psychologist agrees to provide services to a client at the request of a third party, the psychologist assumes the responsibility of clarifying the nature of the relationships to all parties concerned.

c. Where the demands of an organization require psychologists to violate these Ethical Principles, psychologists clarify the nature of the conflict between the demand and these principles. They inform all parties of psychologists' ethical responsibilities and take appropriate action.

d. Psychologists make advance financial arrangements that safeguard the best interest of and are clearly understood by their clients. They neither give nor receive any remuneration for referring clients for professional services. They contribute a portion of their services to work for which they receive little or no financial return.

e. Psychologists terminate a clinical or consulting relationship when it is reasonably clear that the consumer is not benefiting from it. They offer to help the consumer locate alternative sources of assistance.

Appendix 4.7
Telephone Contact Sheet for the Coping with Depression Course

1. First, I would like to ask where you heard about the course (check all of the categories below that apply).

Newspaper:

story _____   Bus Poster _____

advertisement_____   Flyer—where? _____

Student Newspaper:

story _____   Friend _____

advertisement_____   Professional:

Television: medical doctor _____

program _____   therapist _____

public service   minister _____
announcement _____   Other _____

2. Do you know what the course is about? (If not, then give the following information.)

   a. The course teaches skills that are useful for coping with depression. It uses a textbook and a workbook. The homework assignments are designed to help you practice the skills that are covered in the course.

   b. The course is eight weeks long and consists of 12 sessions. The sessions are scheduled twice each week for four weeks, then once each week for the last four weeks.

   c. There are usually six to eight people in a class; classes meet for two hours in the evenings or on Saturday mornings.

   d. Instructors are advanced graduate students in Clinical Psychology and Counseling under the supervision of Dr. _____.

e. The course is offered at several locations:

_____

_____

f. The cost varies from $100 to $150 depending upon family income. Up to one-half of the fee can be earned back by participating in interviews and filling out questionnaires for research purposes. Thus, the fee is essentially $50 to $75. Some health insurance companies will cover the cost of the treatment program.

3. Does this sound like something that you would be interested in doing? If so, you will be called within a week or two to schedule an interview. During the interview we will explain about the course in more detail; we will also want to obtain some information about you so that we can determine whether the course will be helpful for you. IT WILL TAKE 2 TO 2½ HOURS TO COMPLETE THE INTERVIEW.

- -

COVER THE INFORMATION ABOVE
BEFORE COMPLETING THIS FORM

Time _____ Date _____ Person taking call _____

Name of caller: _____ Sex ____ Age ____

Address _____ Zip _____

Home Phone _____ Work Phone _____

Best time to call _____

Additional notes:

Appendix 4.8
Statement of Informed Consent

It is our policy that participants in a research study be fully informed of the procedures we intend to use. Please read the following and sign the Statement of Informed Consent if you are satisfied that you understand the procedures and desire to participate in the program. If you have any questions, please do not hesitate to ask.

General Description

Depression is a common problem in our society. We see depression as primarily being due to the "problems of living" that many of us experience, rather than due to some disease or illness. Among other things, we believe that depressed individuals can learn skills which will help them to cope more effectively with their life problems and thus, with their depression.

We are currently conducting a study of the effectiveness of our approach in helping people cope with their depression. During the program, participants will learn the following skills: relaxation training, self-change techniques, constructive thinking, balancing positive and negative thoughts, effective planning for pleasant activities, and creative use of social skills. Other procedures may be recommended as deemed necessary.

Participants will be assigned to groups as they are available. Groups will begin sometime within one to six weeks after this interview. If we are unable to place you in a group immediately, you will receive a confirmed place in the next group. If, while you are waiting for the next group to begin, you feel the need to consult with our program, you may call us at 686-4966 and we will arrange a meeting.

Assessment Procedures

In order to evaluate your progress in the program, you will be asked to complete various self-report questionnaires and participate in three personal interviews (prior to the program, and one month and six months after the end of the program). You will be asked to complete the self-report measures at the initial interview, at the initial session with your instructor, at the end of the course, and at the one-month and six-month follow-up periods. In addition, very short questionnaires will be completed during some course sessions. The initial interview should take about two hours; the one-month and six-month interviews will be shorter.

Fees

Participants will be charged either $100 or $150 for the entire eight-week program (individual and group), depending on their family income and their number of dependents claimed. Participants may earn back as much as one-half of their fee by complying with the assessment procedures described above. This amount, either $50 or $75, can be earned back in increments for participating during the following assessment periods:

Assessment period:	Percent of refund ($50 or $75) earned:
Initial session w/instructor	20% ($10 or $15)
End of program	20% ($10 or $15)
One-month follow-up (including interview)	20% ($10 or $15)
Six-month follow-up (including interview)	40% ($20 or $30)

All money that is earned back by a participant will be returned in one payment, subsequent to the six-month assessment.

All participants will be required to pay the entire fee at a meeting which will be arranged between the instructor and participant, prior to the beginning of the program.

Any participant may withdraw from the program at any time. The participants will still be required to participate in the assessment procedures in order to earn back (up to) one-half of their fee. The other one-half of the fee will be returned to them on a prorated basis, depending on how much of the program has transpired prior to their notifying the instructor of their intent to withdraw. This notification must be in writing. The price of the text ($6.95) will not be refunded.

Risks and Safeguards

In any study of feelings of depression there exists the potential for hindering as well as aiding psychological progress. There is, therefore, inevitably such a risk in this study. In order to minimize this risk, all staff members are closely supervised and are under the direction of Dr. _____ _____. The techniques used by the staff members are based upon well established practices and are known to be among the safest clinical techniques available.

Since the program involves having you rate and monitor the occurrence of unpleasant or aversive events, as well as pleasant events and moods, there is a risk that this process will remind you of these events and cause you to have some negative feelings. In addition, because the information which staff members obtain in the course of talking with you and having you fill out various forms will be of a personal, confidential, or possibly incriminating nature, the staff members will not divulge such information to anyone other than authorized members of the project staff. Published research data will be presented in such a way that your identity will not be revealed. All written information will be kept in locked files.

Rights of Participants

1. A participant may stop participating in the program at any time simply by notifying his or her interviewer (during the interview), group instructor, or individual therapist. However, to receive a refund, this notification of intent to withdraw must be in writing.
2. A participant may refuse to discuss any matter at any time.
3. A participant may ask questions about the procedures at any time; any reasonable questions of this nature will be answered. However, questions which reveal the precise nature of any hypotheses under study will not be answered until the end of the program.
4. Interviews, class or individual sessions may be recorded and/or observed by the staff. Participants will be informed whenever such procedures are in effect.

STATEMENT OF INFORMED CONSENT

I have read and understand the above statement and I voluntarily agree to participate in this research study as a participant in the Coping with Depression program.

Signature of participant: _____ Date: _____

Signature of witness: _____

Registration fee: _____

Appendix 5.1

The Schedule for Affective Disorders and Schizophrenia—Lifetime version (SADS-L) can be obtained by writing to:

Dr. Jean Endicott
Research Assessment and Training Department
New York State Psychiatric Unit
722 West 168th Street
New York, NY 10032

Appendix 5.2
Diagnostic Criteria
for Unipolar and Bipolar Depressions
(Adapted from DSM-III, American Psychiatric Association, 1980)

I. Unipolar Depressions.

   A. Episodic/Major Depressive Disorder.

      1. Symptoms:

         a. Dysphoria.

         b. At least four of the following: appetite change; sleep difficulties; psychomotor agitation or retardation; loss of pleasure or interest; loss of energy, fatigue; feelings of worthlessness, self-reproach or guilt; concentration difficulties; recurrent thoughts of death or suicide.

      2. Duration: Every day for at least two weeks.

      3. Exclusion criteria: Mood-incongruent delusions or hallucinations; bizarre behavior; schizophrenia, schizophreniform disorder; paranoid disorder; organic mental disorder.

   B. Chronic/Dysthymic Disorder.

      1. Symptoms:

         a. Depressed mood.

         b. At least three of the following: sleep difficulties; low energy level or chronic tiredness; feelings of inadequacy; loss of self-esteem or self-deprecation; decreased effectiveness or productivity; decreased attention or concentration; social withdrawal; loss of interest or enjoyment; irritability or excessive anger; dehedonia; pessimism; tearfulness or crying; recurrent thoughts of death or suicide.

      2. Duration: Most or all of the time during the past two years.

      3. Exclusion criteria: Psychotic features.

   C. Atypical Depression.

      1. Symptoms: Same as major or dysthymic depression.

      2. Duration: Variable.

      3. Exclusion criteria: Adjustment disorder.

II. Bipolar Depressions.

   A. Bipolar Disorder-Depressed/Mixed.

      1. Symptoms:

         a. Same as major depressive disorder.

         b. Mania.

            1) Elevated, expansive or irritable mood, and

            2) At least three of the following: increased activity; talkative; flight of ideas or racing thoughts; inflated self-esteem; decreased need for sleep; distractability; excessive activity without awareness of negative consequences.

      2. Duration: Most of the time during at least one week.

      3. Exclusion criteria: Same as major depressive disorder.

   B. Cyclothymic.

      1. Symptoms:

         a. Depressive periods with:

            1) Depressed mood, and

            2) At least three of the following: sleep difficulties; low energy or chronic fatigue; feelings of inadequacy; decreased effectiveness or productivity; decreased concentration; social withdrawal; loss of interest or pleasure in sex; restricted activities or guilt over past activities; feeling slowed down; less talkative than usual; pessimism; tearfulness or crying.

         b. Hypomanic periods with:

            1) Elevated, expansive or irritable mood, and

            2) At least three of the following: decreased need for sleep; more energy than usual; increased productivity; unusually creative thinking; extreme gregariousness; hypersexuality; excessive activity without awareness of negative consequences; physical restlessness; more talkative than usual; over-optimistic; inappropriate laughing, joking, or punning.

      2. Duration: Two years. Depressive and hypomanic periods may be separated by intervals of normal mood, may be intermixed, or may alternate.

      3. Exclusion criteria: Psychotic features attributed to other mental disorders.

Appendix 5.3

The Research Diagnostic Criteria (RDC) can be obtained by writing to:

Dr. Jean Endicott
Research Assessment and Training Department
New York State Psychiatric Unit
722 West 168th Street
New York, NY 10032

Appendix 5.4
Short Version
of the "Feelings and Concerns Checklist"
(Adapted from Grinker, et al., 1961)

Date: _____

Participant's name: _____   Interview: _____

0 = not present
1 = present to slight extent
2 = present to moderate extent
3 = present to marked extent

1.	Feels hopeless	0	1	2	3
2.	Feels that he or she is bearing troubles	0	1	2	3
3.	Feels helpless and powerless	0	1	2	3
4.	Has feelings of tenseness	0	1	2	3
5.	Concerned with suffering that he or she has caused others	0	1	2	3
6.	Feels problems would be relieved by the solving of certain "material" problems (e.g., money, job)	0	1	2	3
7.	Feels sad and blue	0	1	2	3
8.	Feels self unworthy	0	1	2	3
9.	Considers self lazy	0	1	2	3
10.	Expresses concern for the welfare of family and friends	0	1	2	3
11.	Has ideas of committing suicide	0	1	2	3
12.	Concerned with material loss (e.g., money, property)	0	1	2	3
13.	Feels at "end of rope"	0	1	2	3
14.	Feels envious of others	0	1	2	3
15.	Experiences free anxiety	0	1	2	3
16.	Feels a failure	0	1	2	3
17.	Concerned with making up for wrongs he or she has caused to others	0	1	2	3

18. Uses depressive behavior for interpersonal gains   0 1 2 3

19. Feels guilt for not assuming family, job, and/or academic responsibilities   0 1 2 3

20. Feels unable to make decisions   0 1 2 3

21. Feels unloved   0 1 2 3

22. Feels burdened by the demands of others   0 1 2 3

23. Feels "jittery"   0 1 2 3

24. Feels unable to act   0 1 2 3

25. Credits problems to excessive family and/or job responsibilities   0 1 2 3

26. Depression is the presenting syndrome—5
Patient manifests other symptoms but depression is major—4
Depression is about equal with other symptoms—3
Depression is present but the major symptom is something else—2
Depression is not among the presenting symptoms—1
There are no significant presenting symptoms—0

Factor 1 score =
   Items $1 + 3 + 7 + 8 + 9 + 13$
   $+ 16 + 20 + 24 =$ _____ $\div 9 =$ _____ Dysphoria
Factor 2 score = Items $6 + 12 + 22 + 25 =$ _____ $\div 4 =$ _____ Material burden
Factor 3 score = Items $5 + 10 + 17 + 19 =$ _____ $\div 4 =$ _____ Guilt
Factor 5 score = Items $2 + 14 + 18 + 21 =$ _____ $\div 4 =$ _____ Social isolation

Grand total = _____   Overall mean = Grand total $\div 21 =$ _____

Appendix 5.5
Beck Depression Inventory

(from Beck et al., *Archives of General Psychiatry,* 1961, 4, 561-571.
Copyright 1961, American Medical Association.)

INSTRUCTIONS: This is a questionnaire. On the questionnaire are groups of statements. Please read the entire group of statements in each category. Then pick out the one statement in the group which best describes the way you feel *today,* that is, right now. Circle the number beside the statement you have chosen. If several statements in the group seem to apply equally well, circle each one.

Be sure to read all the statements in the group before making your choice.

A. 0 I do not feel sad.
  1 I feel blue or sad.
  2a I am blue or sad all the time and I can't snap out of it.
  2b I am so sad or unhappy that it is quite painful.
  3 I am so sad or unhappy that I can't stand it.

B. 0 I am not particularly pessimistic or discouraged about the future.
  1 I feel discouraged about the future.
  2a I feel I have nothing to look forward to.
  2b I feel that I won't ever get over my troubles.
  3 I feel that the future is hopeless and that things cannot improve.

C. 0 I do not feel like a failure.
  1 I feel I have failed more than the average person.
  2a I feel I have accomplished very little that is worthwhile or that means anything.
  2b As I look back on my life all I can see is a lot of failure.
  3 I feel I am a complete failure as a person (parent, spouse).

D. 0 I am not particularly dissatisfied.
  1 I feel bored most of the time.
  2a I don't enjoy things the way I used to.
  2b I don't get satisfaction out of anything any more.
  3 I am dissatisfied with everything.

E. 0 I don't feel particularly guilty.
1 I feel bad or unworthy a good part of the time.
2a I feel quite guilty.
2b I feel bad or unworthy practically all the time now.
3 I feel as though I am very bad or worthless.

F. 0 I don't feel I am being punished.
1 I have a feeling that something bad may happen to me.
2 I feel I am being punished or will be punished.
3a I feel I deserve to be punished.
3b I want to be punished.

G. 0 I don't feel disappointed in myself.
1a I am disappointed in myself.
1b I don't like myself.
2 I am disgusted with myself.
3 I hate myself.

H. 0 I don't feel I am worse than anybody else.
1 I am critical of myself for my weakness or mistakes.
2 I blame myself for my faults.
3 I blame myself for everything bad that happens.

I. 0 I don't have any thoughts of harming myself.
1 I have thoughts of harming myself but I would not carry them out.
2a I feel I would be better off dead.
2b I feel my family would be better off if I were dead.
3a I have definite plans about committing suicide.
3b I would kill myself if I could.

J. 0 I don't cry any more than usual.
1 I cry more than I used to.
2 I cry all the time now. I can't stop it.
3 I used to be able to cry but now I can't cry at all even though I want to.

K. 0 I am no more irritated now than I ever am.
1 I get annoyed or irritated more easily than I used to.
2 I feel irritated all the time.
3 I don't get irritated at all at things that used to irritate me.

L. 0 I have not lost interest in other people.
1 I am less interested in other people now than I used to be.
2 I have lost most of my interest in other people and have little feeling for them.
3 I have lost all my interest in other people and don't care about them at all.

M. 0 I make decisions about as well as ever.
1 I try to put off making decisions.
2 I have great difficulty in making decisions.
3 I can't make any decisions at all any more.

N. 0 I don't feel I look any worse than I used to.
1 I am worried that I am looking old or unattractive.
2 I feel that there are permanent changes in my appearance and they make me look unattractive.
3 I feel that I am ugly or repulsive looking.

O. 0 I can work as well as before.
1a It takes extra effort to get started doing something.
1b I don't work as well as I used to.
2 I have to push myself very hard to do anything.
3 I can't do any work at all.

P. 0 I can sleep as well as usual.
1 I wake up more tired in the morning than I used to.
2 I wake up 1-2 hours earlier than usual and find it hard to get back to sleep.
3 I wake up early every day and can't get more than 5 hours sleep.

Q. 0 I don't get any more tired than usual.
1 I get tired more easily than I used to.
2 I get tired from doing anything.
3 I get too tired to do anything.

R. 0 My appetite is no worse than usual.
1 My appetite is not as good as it used to be.
2 My appetite is much worse now.
3 I have no appetite at all any more.

S. 0 I haven't lost much weight, if any, lately.
1 I have lost more than 5 pounds.
2 I have lost more than 10 pounds.
3 I have lost more than 15 pounds.

T. 0 I am no more concerned
about my health than usual.
1 I am concerned about aches
and pains or upset stomach
and constipation.
2 I am so concerned with
how I feel or what I feel
that it's hard to think of
much else.
3 I am completely absorbed in
what I feel.

U. 0 I have not noticed any
recent change in my interest
in sex.
1 I am less interested in sex
than I used to be.
2 I am much less interested in
sex now.
3 I have lost interest in sex
completely.

SCORING

The total score is calculated by
adding together the *highest* number
(0-3) indicated for each group
(A-U).

Range: 0-63

Appendix 5.6
Expected Beck Depression Inventory

(Adapted from Beck et al., *Archives of General Psychiatry*, 1961, 4, 561-571. Copyright 1961, American Medical Association.)

INSTRUCTIONS: This is a questionnaire. On the questionnaire are groups of statements. Please read the entire group of statements in each category. Then pick out the one statement in the group which best describes the way you *expect to feel by the end of the course.* Circle the number beside the statement you have chosen. If several statements in the group seem to apply equally well, circle each one.

Be sure to read all the statements in the group before making your choice.

A. 0 I do not feel sad.
   1 I feel blue or sad.
   2a I am blue or sad all the time and I can't snap out of it.
   2b I am so sad or unhappy that it is quite painful.
   3 I am so sad or unhappy that I can't stand it.

B. 0 I am not particularly pessimistic or discouraged about the future.
   1 I feel discouraged about the future.
   2a I feel I have nothing to look forward to.
   2b I feel that I won't ever get over my troubles.
   3 I feel that the future is hopeless and that things cannot improve.

C. 0 I do not feel like a failure.
   1 I feel I have failed more than the average person.
   2a I feel I have accomplished very little that is worthwhile or that means anything.
   2b As I look back on my life all I can see is a lot of failure.
   3 I feel I am a complete failure as a person (parent, spouse).

D. 0 I am not particularly dissatisfied.
   1 I feel bored most of the time.
   2a I don't enjoy things the way I used to.
   2b I don't get satisfaction out of anything any more.
   3 I am dissatisfied with everything.

E. 0 I don't feel particularly guilty.
1 I feel bad or unworthy a good part of the time.
2a I feel quite guilty.
2b I feel bad or unworthy practically all the time now.
3 I feel as though I am very bad or worthless.

F. 0 I don't feel I am being punished.
1 I have a feeling that something bad may happen to me.
2 I feel I am being punished or will be punished.
3a I feel I deserve to be punished.
3b I want to be punished.

G. 0 I don't feel disappointed in myself.
1a I am disappointed in myself.
1b I don't like myself.
2 I am disgusted with myself.
3 I hate myself.

H. 0 I don't feel I am worse than anybody else.
1 I am critical of myself for my weakness or mistakes.
2 I blame myself for my faults.
3 I blame myself for everything bad that happens.

I. 0 I don't have any thoughts of harming myself.
1 I have thoughts of harming myself but I would not carry them out.
2a I feel I would be better off dead.
2b I feel my family would be better off if I were dead.
3a I have definite plans about committing suicide.
3b I would kill myself if I could.

J. 0 I don't cry any more than usual.
1 I cry more than I used to.
2 I cry all the time now. I can't stop it.
3 I used to be able to cry but now I can't cry at all even though I want to.

K. 0 I am no more irritated now than I ever am.
1 I get annoyed or irritated more easily than I used to.
2 I feel irritated all the time.
3 I don't get irritated at all at things that used to irritate me.

L. 0 I have not lost interest in other people.
1 I am less interested in other people now than I used to be.
2 I have lost most of my interest in other people and have little feeling for them.
3 I have lost all my interest in other people and don't care about them at all.

M. 0 I make decisions about as well as ever.
1 I try to put off making decisions.
2 I have great difficulty in making decisions.
3 I can't make any decisions at all any more.

N. 0 I don't feel I look any worse than I used to.
1 I am worried that I am looking old or unattractive.
2 I feel that there are permanent changes in my appearance and they make me look unattractive.
3 I feel that I am ugly or repulsive looking.

O. 0 I can work as well as before.
1a It takes extra effort to get started doing something.
1b I don't work as well as I used to.
2 I have to push myself very hard to do anything.
3 I can't do any work at all.

P. 0 I can sleep as well as usual.
1 I wake up more tired in the morning than I used to.
2 I wake up 1-2 hours earlier than usual and find it hard to get back to sleep.
3 I wake up early every day and can't get more than 5 hours sleep.

Q. 0 I don't get any more tired than usual.
1 I get tired more easily than I used to.
2 I get tired from doing anything.
3 I get too tired to do anything.

R. 0 My appetite is no worse than usual.
1 My appetite is not as good as it used to be.
2 My appetite is much worse now.
3 I have no appetite at all any more.

S. 0 I haven't lost much weight, if any, lately.
1 I have lost more than 5 pounds.
2 I have lost more than 10 pounds.
3 I have lost more than 15 pounds.

T. 0 I am no more concerned
about my health than usual.

1 I am concerned about aches
and pains or upset stomach
and constipation.

2 I am so concerned with
how I feel or what I feel
that it's hard to think of
much else.

3 I am completely absorbed in
what I feel.

U. 0 I have not noticed any
recent change in my interest
in sex.

1 I am less interested in sex
than I used to be.

2 I am much less interested in
sex now.

3 I have lost interest in sex
completely.

SCORING

The total score is calculated by
adding together the *highest* number
(0–3) indicated for each group
(A–U).

Range: 0–63

Appendix 5.7
CES-D
(from Radloff, 1977)

Circle the number for each statement which best describes how often you felt this way *during the past week*.

DURING THE PAST WEEK:	Rarely or None of the Time (Less than 1 Day)	Some or a Little of the Time (1-2 Days)	Occasionally or a Moderate Amount of Time (3-4 Days)	Most or All of the Time (5-7 Days)
1. I was bothered by things that usually don't bother me	0	1	2	3
2. I did not feel like eating; my appetite was poor	0	1	2	3
3. I felt that I could not shake off the blues even with help from my family or friends	0	1	2	3
4. I felt that I was just as good as other people	0	1	2	3
5. I had trouble keeping my mind on what I was doing	0	1	2	3
6. I felt depressed	0	1	2	3
7. I felt that everything I did was an effort	0	1	2	3
8. I felt hopeful about the future	0	1	2	3
9. I thought my life had been a failure	0	1	2	3
10. I felt fearful	0	1	2	3
11. My sleep was restless	0	1	2	3
12. I was happy	0	1	2	3
13. I talked less than usual	0	1	2	3

14. I felt lonely	0	1	2	3
15. People were unfriendly	0	1	2	3
16. I enjoyed life	0	1	2	3
17. I had crying spells	0	1	2	3
18. I felt sad	0	1	2	3
19. I felt that people disliked me	0	1	2	3
20. I could not "get going"	0	1	2	3

SCORING:

Items 4, 8, 12, and 16 are "reverse items"; score these items as follows: $3 = 0, 2 = 1, 1 = 2, 0 = 3$. The total score is calculated by adding together the score for each item.

Range: 0-60.

Appendix 5.8
Suicide Attempt(s) Interview

Subject No. _____

Date:_____

Interviewer: _____

1. Have you ever considered attempting suicide?
    1 = Yes
    2 = No

2. Have you ever made a suicide attempt?
    1 = Yes
    2 = No

3. How many suicide attempts have you made?
    1 = None
    2 = One
    3 = Two
    4 = Three
    5 = Four or more

4. Probe for the date, circumstances, means, and consequences of each suicide attempt.

    No. 1

    No. 2

    No. 3

    No. 4

Appendix 5.9
Interview Instructions for Social Support Ratings

(Adapted with permission of The Free Press, a Division of MacMillan, Inc. from *Social Origins of Depression* by George W. Brown and Tirril Harris. Copyright ©1978 by George W. Brown and Tirril Harris.)

PART I: This section should be used to determine whether or not the person has a close, intimate relationship with his or her spouse/living partner.

Definition of Intimate Relationship: An "intimate" relationship between two people is assumed to exist when individuals can express their feelings freely and without self-consciousness. For a relationship to provide intimacy there must be trust, effective understanding and ready access. Marriage can provide such a relationship. Occasionally a person may establish a relationship of this kind with a close friend, mother, sister or brother. An intimate relationship does not presuppose a sexual relationship. Communication obviously is an important, but not the only, component. The rating of intimacy should also be based on attitudinal and other general qualities of the relationship.

The interviewer must ask the following questions. In addition, "probes" should be used to elicit further information relevant to each question.

Q1. If you had a problem of some sort, who would be the first person that you would want to discuss it with? This is a "key" question. Record who is mentioned and the nature of the relationship. Encourage the participant to share with you the kind of relationship he or she has with that person, the kinds of problems he or she feels free to discuss, and the kind of behavior he or she anticipates from the other person.

Q2. What about your...husband (pause), mother (pause), sister...father ...brother? What about your friends? Are any of them close enough to you to confide in? Do you feel you could tell them *anything?* Can you share most of the troubles that you might have with them?

Q3. Is your husband (wife, mother, sister, friend, etc.) easy to talk to in general about things? Does he/she ever get bored or stop listening? Does he or she say that you are always worrying about things that aren't really important.

185

Rating Instructions:

A = The participant is considered to have a close, intimate and confiding relationship with a spouse (partner). (Participants should be rated as "A" when, from the information you are eliciting, it is clear that they have a close tie with their spouse even though the spouse was not named as a confidant on the first question.) A participant should also be rated "A" if the relationship is with a same-sex person with whom he or she shares a common domicile, and the relationship has characteristics of a marital tie, i.e., they spend a lot of time talking about mutual problems.

B = The participant does not have an intimate tie with a spouse or partner (or with a person in the same household) but who nevertheless reports having a confiding relationship with someone else, such as a mother, father, sister or friend *whom he or she sees at least weekly.*

C = Participants reporting a confidant who is seen less than weekly.

D = Those who mentioned no one.

PART II. The purpose of this section is to determine whether there have been any *changes* in the social support system of the participant.

1. Number of people in support network. Has there been any change in the *availability* of other people for social interaction as a result of *their* choice or as a result of circumstances beyond your control?

Increase	No change	Decrease
+2 +1	0	−1 −2

2. Amount of social interaction. Has there been any change in the amount of social interaction you have engaged in as a result of *your own choice?*

Increase	No change	Decrease
+2 +1	0	−1 −2

3. Quality of relationships. Has there been any change in the nature of your relationships with any of the people you are close to? Have any of them gone downhill? Have any gotten better? Have there been any major disagreements with any of these people that are still unresolved?

Better   No change   Worse

If there has been a change for the worse, how much has this change bothered you?

Not at all   A little   A lot

4. Amount of emotional support. Has there been any change in the amount of emotional support available (someone to tell your troubles to; someone you have frank, open conversations with; being told you are needed, loved; asking for help or advice; being with people who like and care about you, e.g., friends, grandchildren, etc.).

5. Satisfaction. Find out how satisfied the participant feels about his/her current relationships. Do they feel loved, treated fairly, respected, accepted? Has there been any change since (reference date)?

More Satisfying   Same   Less Satisfying
$+2$ $+1$ 0 -1 -2

Appendix 5.9, continued
Social Support Rating Summary Table

SUBJECT _____

INTERVIEWER _____

DATE _____

Part I. Brown Intimacy Scale (circle one)

A   B   C   D

Use the rest of this page for your notes and a paragraph explaining the basis for your rating.

Part II. Change in social support.

1. Number of people in support network.

     + 2   + 1   0   − 1   − 2

2. Amount of social interaction.

     + 2   + 1   0   − 1   − 2

3. Quality of relationships.

     + 2   + 1   0   − 1   − 2

4. Amount of emotional support.

     + 2   + 1   0   − 1   − 2

5. Satisfaction.

     + 2   + 1   0   − 1   − 2

Appendix 5.10

The Social Adjustment Scale (SAS) can be obtained by writing to:

Myrna M. Weissman, Ph.D.
Depression Research Unit
Department of Psychiatry
Yale University School of Medicine
350 Congress Avenue
New Haven, CT 06519-8068

Appendix 5.11
Medical Condition Interview

Subject No. _____

Date: _____

Interviewer: _____

1. How would you rate your overall health at the present time?

   1 = Excellent
   2 = Good
   3 = Fair
   4 = Poor
   5 = Very poor

2. Do you have any physical handicaps?

   1 = Yes
   2 = No

   What is the nature of the handicap?

3. Do you have any disabling diseases?

   1 = Yes
   2 = No

   What is the nature of the disease?

4. Have you recently undergone surgery?

   1 = Yes
   2 = No

   What was the nature of the surgery?

Appendix 5.12

The Wide Range Achievement Test (WRAT) can be obtained by writing to:

Jastak Associates, Inc.
1526 Gilpin Avenue
Wilmington, Delaware 19806

Appendix 5.13
Specific Areas of Difficulty and Progress Report

Include for each participant the following information:

A. Areas of difficulty.

In this section, note areas of difficulty for the participant; e.g., social interaction, marital problems, physical handicaps, etc. Pinpoint specific problems and/or areas of maladjustment, including hypotheses concerning the onset of a psychiatric disorder.

B. Progress notes.

Note areas of improvement for each participant, as well as new problems and/or episodes of depression that occur during the course.

Appendix 6.1
Relaxation Patter

Relaxation of Arms (time: 4-5 minutes)

Settle back as comfortably as you can. Let yourself relax to the best of your ability.... Now, as you relax like that, clench your right fist, just clench your fist tighter and tighter, and study the tension as you do so. Keep it clenched and feel the tension in your right fist, hand, and forearm...and now relax. Let the fingers of your right hand become loose, and observe the contrast in the way it feels.... Now, let yourself go and try to become more relaxed all over.... Once more, clench your right fist really tight... hold it, and notice the tension again.... Now let go, relax; straighten out your fingers and notice the difference once more.... Now repeat the same procedure with your left fist. Clench your left fist while the rest of your body relaxes; clench that fist tighter and feel the tension...and now relax. Again enjoy the contrast.... Repeat that once more, clench the left fist, tight and tense.... Now do the opposite of tension—relax and feel the difference. Continue relaxing like that for a while.... Clench both fists tighter and tighter, both fists tense, forearms tense, study the sensation... and relax; straighten out your fingers and feel that relaxation. Continue relaxing your hands and forearms more and more.... Now bend your elbows and tense your biceps, tense them harder and study the tension feelings.... All right, straighten out your arms, let them relax and feel that difference again. Let the relaxation develop.... Once more, tense your biceps; hold the tension and observe it carefully.... Straighten the arms and relax; relax to the best of your ability.... Each time, pay close attention to your feelings when you tense up and when you relax. Now straighten your arms, straighten them so that you feel the most tension in the triceps along the back of your arms; stretch your arms and feel that tension...and now relax. Get your arms back into a comfortable position. Let the relaxation proceed on its own. Your arms should feel comfortably heavy as you allow them to relax.... Straighten your arms once more so that you feel the tension in the triceps; straighten them. Feel that tension...and relax. Now let's concentrate on pure relaxation in the arms without any tension. Make your arms comfortable and let them relax further and further. Continue relaxing your arms even further. Even when your arms seem fully relaxed, try to go that extra bit further; try to achieve deeper and deeper levels of relaxation.

194

Relaxation of Facial Area with Neck, Shoulders, and Upper Back (time: 4-5 minutes)

Let all your muscles go loose and heavy. Just settle back quietly and comfortably. Wrinkle up your forehead now; wrinkle it tighter. . . . And now stop wrinkling your forehead, relax and smooth it out. Picture your entire forehead and scalp becoming smoother as the relaxation increases. . . . Now frown and crease your brows and study the tension. . . . Let go of the tension again. Smooth out your forehead once more. . . . Now close your eyes tighter and tighter. . . feel the tension. . . and relax your eyes. Keep your eyes closed, gently, comfortably, and notice the relaxation. . . . Now clench your jaws, bite your teeth together; study the tension throughout the jaws. . . . Relax your jaws now. Let your lips part slightly. . . . Appreciate the relaxation. . . . Now press your tongue hard against the roof of your mouth. Look for the tension. . . . All right, let your tongue return to a comfortable and relaxed position. . . . Now purse your lips, press your lips together tighter and tighter. . . . Relax your lips. Note the contrast between tension and relaxation. Feel the relaxation all over your face, all over your forehead and scalp, eyes, jaws, lips, tongue and throat. The relaxation progresses further and further. . . . Now attend to your neck muscles. Press your head back as far as it can go and feel the tension in your neck; roll it to the right and feel the tension shift; now roll it to the left. Straighten your neck and bring your head forward, pressing your chin against your chest. Let your head return to a comfortable position, and study the relaxation. Let the relaxation develop. . . . Now shrug your shoulders. Hold the tension. . . . Drop your shoulders and feel the relaxation. Your neck and shoulders should feel relaxed. . . . Shrug your shoulders again and move them around. Bring your shoulders up, forward, and then back. Feel the tension in your shoulders and in your upper back. . . . Drop your shoulders once more and relax. Let the relaxation spread deep into your shoulders, right into your back muscles; relax your neck and throat, and your jaws and other facial areas as the pure relaxation takes over and grows deeper. . . deeper. . . deeper.

Relaxation of Chest, Stomach and Lower Back (time: 4-5 minutes)

Relax your entire body to the best of your ability. Feel that comfortable heaviness that accompanies relaxation. Breathe easily and freely in and out. Notice how the relaxation increases as you exhale. . . as you breathe out just feel that relaxation. . . . Now breathe in and fill your lungs; inhale deeply and hold your breath. Study the tension. . . . Now exhale, let the walls of your chest grow loose and push the air out automatically. Continue relaxing and breathe freely and gently. Feel the relaxation and enjoy it.... With the rest of your body as relaxed as possible, fill your lungs again. Breathe in deeply and hold it again.... That's fine, breathe out and appreciate the relief. Just breathe normally. Continue relaxing your chest and let the relaxation spread to your back, shoulders, neck and arms. Merely let go ...and enjoy the relaxation. Now let's pay attention to your abdominal muscles, your stomach area. Tighten your stomach muscles, make your abdomen hard. Notice the tension...and relax. Let the muscles loosen and notice the contrast.... Once more, press and tighten your stomach muscles. Hold the tension and study it...and relax. Notice the general well-being that comes with relaxing your stomach.... Now draw your stomach in, pull the muscles in and feel the tension.... Now relax again. Let your stomach out. Continue breathing normally and easily and feel that gentle massaging action all over your chest and stomach.... Now pull your stomach in again and hold the tension.... Now push out and tense; hold the tension...once more pull in and feel the tension...now relax your stomach fully. Let the tension dissolve as the relaxation grows deeper. Each time you breathe out, notice the rhythmic relaxation both in your lungs and in your stomach. Notice how your chest and stomach relax more and more.... Try and let go of all contractions anywhere in your body.... Now direct your attention to your lower back. Arch your back, make your lower back quite hollow, and feel the tension along your spine ...and settle down comfortably again relaxing the lower back.... Now arch your back and feel the tension as you do so. Try to keep the rest of your body as relaxed as possible. Try to localize the tension throughout your lower back area.... Relax once more, relaxing further and further. Relax your lower back, relax your upper back, spread the relaxation to your stomach, chest, shoulders, arms, and facial area. These parts keep relaxing further and further and further and ever deeper.

Relaxation of Hips, Thighs and Calves Followed by Complete Body Relaxation (time: 4-5 minutes)

Let go of all tension and relax.... Now flex your buttocks and thighs. Flex your thighs by pressing down your heels as hard as you can.... Relax and note the difference.... Straighten your knees and flex your thigh muscles again. Hold the tension.... Relax your hips and thighs. Allow the relaxation to proceed on its own.... Press your feet and toes downwards, away from your face, so that your calf muscles become tense. Study that tension.... Relax your feet and calves.... This time, bend your feet towards your face so that you feel tension along your shins. Bring your toes right up...relax again. Keep relaxing for a while.... Now let yourself relax further all over. Relax your feet, ankles, calves and shins, knees, thighs, buttocks and hips. Feel the heaviness of your lower body as you relax still further.... Now spread the relaxation to your stomach, waist, and lower back. Let go more and more. Feel that relaxation all over. Let it proceed to your upper back, chest, shoulders and arms and right to the tips of your fingers. Keep relaxing more and more deeply. Make sure that there is no tension in your throat; relax your neck and your jaws and all your facial muscles. Keep relaxing your whole body like that for a while. Let yourself relax.

Now you can become twice as relaxed as you are by merely taking in a really deep breath and exhaling slowly. With your eyes closed so that you can become less aware of objects and movements around you and thus prevent any surface tensions from developing, breathe in deeply and feel yourself becoming heavier. Take in a long, deep breath and let it out very slowly.... Feel how heavy and relaxed you have become.

In a state of perfect relaxation you should feel unwilling to move a single muscle in your body. Think about the effort that would be required to raise your right arm. As you *think* about raising your right arm, see if you can notice any tension that might have crept into your shoulder and arm.... Now you decide not to lift the arm but to continue relaxing. Observe the relief and the disappearance of the tension....

Just carry on relaxing like that. When you wish to get up, count backwards from four to one. You should then feel refreshed, wide awake and calm.

Appendix 6.2
PES Score Summary Sheet

Client's Name _____

		Client's Pretreatment Scores		Norms on Normals According to Age & Sex*		Client's Post-treatment Scores	
		Mean	S.D.	Mean	S.D.	Mean	S.D.
All Events	Frequency						
	Potential Enjoyment						
	Experienced Pleasure						
Mood Related Events	Frequency						
	Potential Enjoyment						
	Experienced Pleasure						
Solitary Events	Frequency						
	Potential Enjoyment						
	Experienced Pleasure						
Passive Outdoor Events	Frequency						
	Potential Enjoyment						
	Experienced Pleasure						

Sexual Events	Frequency	
	Potential Enjoyment	
	Experienced Pleasure	

Frequency-Enjoyability Correlation	

*Norms are provided in *Control Your Depression* (Table 6-2, page 90). For more extensive norms, please write to:

> Dr. Peter M. Lewinsohn
> University of Oregon/Straub Hall
> Department of Psychology
> Human Neuropsychology Laboratory
> Eugene, OR 97403

SCORING

The "All Events" score can be calculated using the directions given on pages 90-91 in *Control Your Depression*. Note that "Potential Enjoyment" and "Experienced Pleasure" listed above are the same as "Pleasantness" and "Cross-Product" in *Control Your Depression*. To calculate scores for the other categories of events (i.e., Mood Related Events, Solitary Events, Passive Outdoor Events, and Sexual Events) write to Dr. Peter M. Lewinsohn for instructions at the address given above.

Appendix 6.3
Contract Outline

My goal for the next four days is to bring my total pleasant activity count for that period up to _____. This means that I will try to engage in _____ pleasant activities each day. I will also try to keep my pleasant activity level from falling below _____ on any given day.

If my daily total is _____, I will reward myself by _____ . If my total for the four days is _____, I will reward myself by _____ .

Signed _____

Dated _____

Appendix 6.4
Structure for Reward Menu

A. People: List two people with whom you would like to spend more time each week but don't get a chance to.

    1. _____

    2. _____

B. Places: List two places where you would like to spend more time, but don't get a chance to.

    1. _____

    2. _____

C. Things: List two things you do not own that you would most like to have and can afford (book, album, new shoes, etc.).

    1. _____

    2. _____

List your four best liked foods and drinks. You may also want to include items that you do not have very often.

    1. _____

    2. _____

    3. _____

    4. _____

D. Activities: List two activities you would like to engage in more than you do now.

    1. _____

    2. _____

E. Now select from above the three rewards that are the most powerful for you.

    1. _____

    2. _____

    3. _____

Appendix 6.5
Ellis's Ten Major Irrational Beliefs

1. I *must* have love or approval from all the people I find significant.

2. I must prove thoroughly adequate, competent and achieving.

3. When people act obnoxiously or unfairly, I should blame them and see them as wicked individuals.

4. When I get frustrated, rejected, or treated unfairly, I must view things as awful, terrible, or catastrophic.

5. Emotional misery comes from external pressures and I have little ability to control or change my feelings.

6. If something seems dangerous or fearsome, I must preoccupy myself with it and feel anxious about it.

7. I can more easily avoid facing many life difficulties and self-responsibilities than undertake more rewarding forms of self-discipline.

8. Because something strongly influenced my life in the past, it has to keep determining my feelings and behavior today.

9. People and things should turn out better than they do and I must view it as awful and horrible if I do not find good solutions to life's grim realities.

10. I can achieve maximum happiness by inertia and inaction or by passively and uncommittedly "enjoying myself."

From: Ellis, A. & Harper, R. *A New Guide to Rational Living*. Hollywood, California: Wilshire Book Company, 1975. Copyright by Institute for Rational Emotive Therapy; reprinted with permission.

About the Authors

PETER M. LEWINSOHN, PH.D. is a Professor of Psychology and Director of the Geropsychological Services Program at the University of Oregon in Eugene. A Diplomate in Clinical Psychology of the American Board of Professional Psychology, he is well known for his work on the behavioral assessment and treatment of clinical depression. Dr. Lewinsohn has published over 100 articles and book chapters and is the senior author of *Control Your Depression* (with R.F. Muñoz, M.A. Youngren, & A.M. Zeiss, Englewood Cliffs, N.J.: Prentice-Hall, 1986) and *Clinical Geropsychology* (with L. Teri, New York: Pergamon Press, 1983).

DAVID O. ANTONUCCIO, PH.D. is a clinical psychologist and Assistant Coordinator of the Mental Hygiene Clinic at the Veterans Administration Medical Center in Reno, Nevada. He is also an Assistant Professor in the Department of Psychiatry and Behavioral Sciences at the University of Nevada—Reno School of Medicine. He received his B.A. (with honors) in Psychology and Economics from Stanford University in 1975, and his M.A. (1979) and Ph.D. (1980) in Clinical Psychology from the University of Oregon. Dr. Antonuccio has numerous publications on the treatment of depression and on cigarette smoking behavior.

JULIA STEINMETZ BRECKENRIDGE, PH.D. (formerly Julia Steinmetz) is a clinical psychologist and Coordinator of the Center for the Study of Psychotherapy and Aging at the Veterans Administration Medical Center, Palo Alto, California. She received her B.A. (1974) from Stanford University, and her M.A. (1978) and Ph.D. (1981) from the University of Oregon. Dr. Breckenridge has published numerous articles and chapters on the assessment and treatment of depression in both younger and older adults.

LINDA TERI, PH.D. is an Assistant Professor in the Department of Psychiatry and Behavioral Sciences and Chief Psychologist of the Geriatric and Family Services Clinic at the University of Washington Medical School in Seattle. Since receiving her doctorate in Psychology from the University of Vermont in 1980, she has been actively engaged in teaching, research, clinical work and supervision in the areas of depression and geropsychology. Dr. Teri is the author of numerous professional papers and publications and is co-author of *Clinical Geropsychology* (with P.M. Lewinsohn, New York: Pergamon Press, 1983).

References

Alberti, R.E., & Emmons, M.L. *Your perfect right*. San Luis Obispo, California: Impact Publishers, 1982.

Amenson, C.S. & Lewinsohn, P.M. An investigation into the observed sex differences in prevalence of unipolar depression. *Journal of Abnormal Psychology*, 1981, *90*, 1-13.

American Psychiatric Association. *The diagnostic and statistical manual of mental disorders, Third edition*. Washington, D.C.: APA, 1980.

American Psychological Association. Ethical principles of psychologists. *American Psychologist*, 1981, 633-638.

Antonuccio, D.O., Akins, W.T., Chatham, P., Tearnan, B. & Ziegler, B. *An exploratory study: The psychoeducational group treatment of chronically depressed veterans*. Reno, Nevada: Veteran's Administration Medical Center, 1982.

Antonuccio, D.O., Akins, W.T., Chatham, P., Monagin, J., Tearnan, B., & Ziegler, B. An exploratory study: The psychoeducational group treatment of drug-refractory unipolar depression. *Journal of Behavior Therapy and Experimental Psychiatry*, 1984, in press.

Antonuccio, D.O., Lewinsohn, P.M., & Steinmetz, J.L. Identification of therapist differences in a group treatment for depression. *Journal of Consulting and Clinical Psychology,* 1982, *50,* 433-435.

Bandura, A. *Social learning theory.* Englewood Cliffs, New Jersey: Prentice-Hall, 1977.

Beck, A.T. *Depression: Clinical, experimental, and theoretical aspects.* New York: Harper & Row, 1967.

Beck, A.T., Rush, A.J., Shaw, B.F. & Emery, G. *Cognitive therapy of depression: A treatment manual.* New York: Guilford Press, 1979.

Beck, A.T., Ward, C.H., Mendelson, M., Mock, J., & Erbaugh, J. An inventory for measuring depression. *Archives of General Psychiatry,* 1961, *4,* 561-571.

Becker, J. *Depression: Theory and research.* New York: V.H. Winston & Sons, 1974.

Bellack, A.S., Hersen, M., & Himmelhoch, J. Social skills training, pharmacotherapy, and psychotherapy for unipolar depression. *American Journal of Psychiatry,* 1981, *138,* 1562-1567.

Bem, S.L. The measurement of psychological androgyny. *Journal of Consulting and Clinical Psychology,* 1974, *42,* 155-182.

Benson, H. *The relaxation response.* New York: William Morrow, 1975.

Bisno, B., Thompson, L.W., Breckenridge, J.N., & Gallagher, D. *Cognitive predictors of outcome for older adults participating in a psychoeducational program for the treatment of depression.* Paper presented at the Western Psychological Association, 1982.

Bloom, L.Z., Coburn, K., & Pearlman, J. *The new assertive woman.* New York: Dell Publishing Company, 1975.

Brown, G.W., & Harris, T. *Social origins of depression.* New York: The Free Press, 1978.

Brown, R. & Lewinsohn, P.M. *Participant workbook for the coping with depression course.* Eugene, Oregon: Castalia Publishing Company, 1984a.

Brown, R., & Lewinsohn, P.M. A psychoeducational approach to the treatment of depression: Comparison of group, individual, and minimal contact procedures. *Journal of Consulting and Clinical Psychology,* 1984b, in press.

Burglass, D., & Horton, J. A scale for predicting subsequent suicidal behavior. *British Journal of Psychiatry,* 1974, *124,* 573-578.

Cohen, J. A coefficient of agreement for nominal scales. *Educational and Psychological Measurement,* 1960, *20,* 37-46.

Ellis, A., & Harper, R.A. *A new guide to rational living.* Hollywood, California: Wilshire Book Company, 1975.

Endicott, J., & Spitzer, R.L. A diagnostic interview: The schedule for affective disorders and schizophrenia. *Archives of General Psychiatry,* 1978, *35,* 837-844.

Ernst, P., Badash, D., Beran, B., Kosovsky, R., & Kleinhauz, M. Incidence of mental illness in the aged: Unmasking the effect of a diagnosis of chronic brain syndrome. *Journal of the American Geriatric Society,* 1977, *25,* 371-375.

Flanders, N.A. *Analyzing teacher behavior.* Reading, Mass.: Addison-Wesley, 1970.

Flowers, J.V., & Booraem, C.D. Three studies toward a fuller understanding of behavior group therapy: Cohesion, client flexibility and outcome generalization. In D. Upper & S.M. Ross (Eds.), *Behavioral group therapy, 1980: An annual review.* Champaign, Illinois: Research Press, 1980.

Flowers, J.V., Booraem, C.D., & Hartmann, K.A. Clients' improvement on higher and lower intensity problems as a function of group cohesiveness. *Psychotherapy: Theory, Research, and Practice,* 1981, *18,* 246-251.

Frazer, A. Biological aspects of mania and depression. In A. Frazer & A. Winokur (Eds.), *Biological bases of psychiatric disorders.* New York: Spectrum Publications, 1977.

Fuchs, C.Z., & Rehm, L.P. A self-control behavior therapy program for depression. *Journal of Consulting and Clinical Psychology,* 1977, *45,* 206-215.

Garfield, S.L. Research on client variables in psychotherapy. In S.L. Garfield & A.E. Bergin (Eds.), *Handbook of psychotherapy and behavior change: An empirical analysis* (2nd edition). New York: John Wiley & Sons, 1978.

Gonzales, L., Lewinsohn, P.M., Teri, L., & Clarke, G. *Long term follow-up of coping with depression course participants.* University of Oregon, in preparation.

Grinker, R.R., Miller, J., Sabshin, M., Nunn, R., & Nunnally, J.C. *The phenomena of depressions.* New York: Paul B. Hoeber, 1961.

Grosscup, S., & Lewinsohn, P.M. Unpleasant and pleasant events and mood. *Journal of Clinical Psychology,* 1980, *36,* 252-259.

Gurland, B.J. The comparative frequency of depression in various adult age groups. *Journal of Gerontology,* 1976, *31,* 283-292.

Hall, R.C., Popkin, M.K., Devaul, R.A., Faillance, L.A., & Stickney, S.K. Physical illness presenting as psychiatric disease. *Archives of General Psychiatry,* 1978, *35,* 1315-1320.

Hamilton, M.A. A rating scale for depression. *Journal of Neurology, Neurosurgery, and Psychiatry,* 1960, *23,* 56-61.

Hirschfeld, R.M.A., Klerman, G.L., Chodoff, P., Korchin, S., & Barret, J. Dependency, self-esteem, clinical depression. *Journal of the American Academy of Psychoanalysis,* 1976, *4,* 373-388.

Hoberman, H., Lewinsohn, P.M., & Tilson, M. *Predictors of treatment response in the coping with depression course.* University of Oregon, in preparation.

Hollon, S.D., & Beck, A.T. Psychotherapy and drug therapy: Comparisons and combinations. In S.L. Garfield & A.E. Bergin (Eds.), *The handbook of psychotherapy and behavior change: An empirical analysis* (2nd edition). New York: John Wiley & Sons, 1978.

Holmes, T.H., & Rahe, R.H. The social readjustment rating scale. *Psychosomatic Medicine,* 1967, *11,* 213-218.

Jacobsen, E. *Progressive relaxation.* Chicago: University of Chicago Press, 1929.

Jastak, J.F., & Jastak, S. *The wide range achievement test.* Wilmington, Delaware: Jastak Associates, 1978.

Johnson, S. *First person singular.* New York: J.B. Lippincott Company, 1977.

Keller, M.B., & Shapiro, R.W. Major depressive disorder: Initial results from a one year prospective naturalistic follow-up study. *Journal of Nervous and Mental Disorders,* 1981, *169,* 761-768.

Kranzler, G. *You can change how you feel.* Eugene, Oregon: RETC Press, 1974.

Lehman, H.E. Epidemiology of depressive disorders. In R.R. Fieve (Ed.), *Depression in the 70's: Modern theory and research.* Princeton, New Jersey: Excerpta Medica, 1971.

Lettieri, D.F. Research issues in developing prediction scales. In C. Neuringer (Ed.), *Psychological assessment of suicidal risk.* Springfield, Illinois: Charles C. Thomas, 1974.

Lewinsohn, P.M. Engagement in pleasant activities and depression level. *Journal of Abnormal Psychology,* 1975, *84*(6), 729-731.

Lewinsohn, P.M. Manual of instruction for behavior ratings used for observation of interpersonal behavior. In E.J. Mash & L.G. Terdal (Eds.), *Behavior therapy assessment.* New York: Springer Publishing Company, 1976.

Lewinsohn, P.M., Fenn, D.J., & Franklin, J. *The relationship of age of onset to duration of episode in unipolar depression.* Unpublished mimeograph, University of Oregon, 1982.

Lewinsohn, P.M., & Graf, M. Pleasant activities and depression. *Journal of Consulting and Clinical Psychology,* 1973, *41,* 261-268.

Lewinsohn, P.M., & Hoberman, H. Behavioral and cognitive approaches to treatment. In E.S. Paykel (Ed.), *Handbook of affective disorders.* Edinburgh: Churchill-Livingston, 1982.

Lewinsohn, P.M., & Lee, W.M.L. Assessment of affective disorders. In D.H. Barlow (Ed.), *Behavioral assessment of adult disorders.* New York: Guilford Press, 1981.

Lewinsohn, P.M., Mermelstein, R.M., Alexander, C., & MacPhillamy, D.J. The unpleasant events schedule: A scale for the measurement of aversive events. *Journal of Applied Psychological Measurement,* 1984, in press.

Lewinsohn, P.M., Muñoz, R.F., Youngren, M.A., & Zeiss, A.M. *Control your depression.* Englewood Cliffs, New Jersey: Prentice-Hall, 1986.

Lewinsohn, P.M., Sullivan, J.M., & Grosscup, S.J. Changing reinforcing events: An approach to the treatment of depression. *Psychotherapy: Theory, Research, and Practice,* 1980, *17,* 322-334.

Lewinsohn, P.M., Sullivan, J.M., & Grosscup, S.J. Behavioral therapy: Clinical applications. In A.J. Rush (Ed.), *Short term psychotherapies for the depressed patient.* New York: Guilford Press, 1982.

Lewinsohn, P.M., & Talkington, J. Studies on the measurement of unpleasant events and relations with depression. *Applied Psychological Measurement,* 1979, *3,* 83-101.

Lewinsohn, P.M., & Teri, L. Selection of depressed and nondepressed subjects on the basis of self-report data. *Journal of Consulting and Clinical Psychology,* 1982, *50,* 590-591.

Lewinsohn, P.M., Teri, L., & Hoberman, H. Depression: A perspective on etiology, treatment, and life span issues. In M. Rosenbaum, C. Franks, & Y. Jaffe (Eds.), *Perspectives on behavior therapy in the eighties.* New York: Springer Publishing Company, 1983.

Lewinsohn, P.M., Youngren, M.A., & Grosscup, S.J. Reinforcement and depression. In R.A. Depue (Ed.), *The psychobiology of depressive disorders: Implications for the effects of stress.* New York: Academic Press, 1979.

Lieberman, M.A., Yalom, I.D., & Miles, M. *Encounter groups: First facts.* New York: Basic Books, 1973.

Lubin, B. Adjective checklists for measurement of depression. *Archives of General Psychiatry,* 1965, *12,* 57-62.

MacPhillamy, D.J., & Lewinsohn, P.M. *A scale for the measurement of positive reinforcement.* Unpublished mimeograph, University of Oregon, 1971.

MacPhillamy, D.J., & Lewinsohn, P.M. The pleasant events schedule: Studies on reliability, validity, and scale intercorrelation. *Journal of Consulting and Clinical Psychology,* 1982, *50*(3), 363-380.

McLean, P.D., & Hakstian, A.R. Clinical depression: Comparative efficacy of outpatient treatments. *Journal of Consulting and Clinical Psychology,* 1979, *47,* 818-836.

Mendels, J. (Ed.). *The psychobiology of depression.* New York: Spectrum Publications, 1975.

Miles, P.C. Condition predisposing to suicide: A review. *Journal of Nervous and Mental Disease,* 1977, *164,* 231-256.

Morris, J.B., & Beck, A.T. The efficacy of anti-depressant drugs: A review of research (1958 to 1972). *Archives of General Psychiatry,* 1974, *30,* 667-674.

Myers, S.K., & Weissman, M.M. Use of a self-report symptom scale to detect depression in a community sample. *American Journal of Psychiatry,* 1980, *137,* 1081-1084.

Parloff, M.B., Wolfe, B., Hadley, S., & Waskow, I. *Assessment of psychosocial treatment of mental disorders: Current status and prospects.* Unpublished mimeograph, 1978.

Patterson, W.M., Dohn, H.H., Bird, J., & Patterson, G.A. Evaluation of suicidal patients: The SAD PERSONS scale. *Journal of the Academy of Psychosomatic Medicine,* 1983, *24,* 343-349.

Radloff, L.S. The CES-D scale: A self-report depression scale for research in the general population. *Applied Psychological Measurement,* 1977, *1*(3), 385-401.

Raskin, A., & Jarvik, L.F. (Eds.). *Psychiatric symptoms and cognitive loss in the elderly.* Washington, D.C.: Hemisphere Publications, 1979.

Rehm, L.P. *Behavior therapy for depression.* New York: Academic Press, 1981.

Rehm, L.P., & Kornblith, S.J. Behavior therapy for depression: A review of recent developments. In M. Hersen, R.M. Eisler, & P.M. Miller (Eds.), *Progress in behavior modification.* New York: Academic Press, 1979.

Reisinger, J.J. The treatment of "anxiety-depression" via positive reinforcement and response contingency. *Journal of Applied Behavior Analysis,* 1972, *5,* 125-130.

Robins, E., & Guze, S.B. Classification of affective disorders: The primary-secondary, the endogenous-reactive, and the neurotic-psychotic concepts. In T.A. Williams et al. (Eds.), *Recent advances in the psychobiology of the depressive illnesses.* Chevy-Chase, Maryland: U.S. Department of Health, Education, and Welfare, 1969, 283-295.

Robinson, J.C., & Lewinsohn, P.M. An experimental analysis of a technique based on the Premack principle for changing verbal behavior of depressed individuals. *Psychological Reports,* 1973, *32,* 199-210.

Rosen, G.M. *The relaxation book.* Englewood Cliffs, New Jersey: Prentice-Hall, 1977.

Rosenbaum, M. A schedule for assessing self-control behaviors: Preliminary findings. *Behavior Therapy,* 1980, *11,* 109-121.

Rosenshine, B., & Furst, N. Research on teacher performance criteria. In B.O. Smith (Ed.), *Research in teacher education.* Englewood Cliffs, New Jersey: Prentice-Hall, 1971.

Rush, A.J., & Beck, A.T. Behavior therapy in adults with affective disorders. In M. Hersen & A.S. Bellack (Eds.), *Behavior therapy in the psychiatric setting.* Baltimore, Maryland: Williams & Wilkins, 1978.

Rush, A.J., Beck, A.T., Kovacs, M., & Hollon, S. Comparative efficacy of cognitive therapy and imipramine in the treatment of depressed outpatients. *Cognitive Therapy and Research,* 1977, *1,* 17-37.

Sanchez, V.C., Lewinsohn, P.M., & Larson, D. Assertion training: Effectiveness in the treatment of depression. *Journal of Clinical Psychology,* 1980, *36,* 526-529.

Seligman, M.E.P. *Helplessness.* San Francisco: W.H. Freeman, 1975.

Smith, M.J. *When I say no, I feel guilty.* New York: Dial Press, 1975.

Spitzer, R.L., Endicott, J., & Robins, E. Research diagnostic criteria: Rationale and reliability. *Archives of General Psychiatry,* 1978, *35,* 773-782.

Steinbrueck, S.M., Maxwell, S.E., & Howard, G.S. A metaanalysis of psychotherapy and drug therapy in the treatment of unipolar depression with adults. *Journal of Consulting and Clinical Psychology,* 1983, *51*(6), 856-863.

Steinmetz, J.L., Antonuccio, D.O., Bond, M., McKay, G., Brown, R., & Lewinsohn, P.M. *Instructor's manual for the coping with depression course.* Unpublished mimeograph, University of Oregon, 1979.

Steinmetz, J.L., Lewinsohn, P.M., & Antonuccio, D.O. Client variables as predictors of outcome in a structured group treatment for depression. *Journal of Consulting and Clinical Psychology,* 1983, *51*(3), 331-337.

Steinmetz, J.L., Thompson, L.W., Breckenridge, J.N., & Gallagher, D. Behavioral group therapy with the elderly: A psychoeducational approach. In D. Upper & S. Ross (Eds.), *Handbook of behavioral group therapy.* New York: Plenum Press, 1984, in press.

Steinmetz, J.L., Zeiss, A.M., & Thompson, L.W. *The life satisfaction course: An intervention for the elderly.* Paper presented at the NIMH state-of-the-art workshop on the prevention of depression, San Francisco, California, April, 1983.

Strupp, H.H. Success and failure in time-limited psychotherapy. *Archives of General Psychiatry,* 1980, *37,* 708-716, 831-841.

Strupp, H.H., & Hadley, S. Specific vs. nonspecific factors in psychotherapy: A controlled study of outcome. *Archives of General Psychiatry,* 1979, *36,* 1125-1136.

Teri, L., & Leitenberg, H. *Assertion training in the treatment of depression in a community mental health center.* Paper presented at the Association for the Advancement of Behavior Therapy, 1979.

Teri, L., & Lewinsohn, P.M. Modification of the pleasant and unpleasant events schedules for use with the elderly. *Journal of Consulting and Clinical Psychology,* 1982, *50,* 444-445.

Thompson, L.W., Gallagher, D., Nies, G., & Epstein, D. *Evaluation of the effectiveness of professionals and nonprofessionals as instructors of coping with depression classes for elders.* Unpublished mimeograph, University of Southern California and Palo Alto VA Medical Center, 1982.

Turner, R.W., Wehl, C.K., Cannon, D.S., & Craig, K.A. *Individual treatment for depression in alcoholics: A comparison of behavioral, cognitive, and nonspecific therapy.* Unpublished mimeograph, Salt Lake City: Veteran's Administration Medical Center, 1980.

Vaughn, C.E., & Leff, J.P. The measurement of expressed emotion in the families of psychiatric patients. *British Journal of Social and Clinical Psychology,* 1976, *15,* 157-165.

Weissman, M.M., & Klerman, G.L. Sex differences and the epidemiology of depression. *Archives of General Psychiatry,* 1977, *34,* 98-111.

Weissman, M.M., Klerman, G.L., Prusoff, B., Sholomskas, D., & Padin, N. Depressed outpatients one year after treatment with drugs and/or interpersonal therapy. *Archives of General Psychiatry,* 1981, *38,* 51-55.

Weissman, M.M., & Paykel, E.S. *The depressed woman.* Chicago: University of Chicago Press, 1974.

Weissman, M.M., Prusoff, B., & Klerman, G.L. Personality and the prediction of long term outcome of depression. *American Journal of Psychiatry,* 1978, *105,* 797-800.

Wills, T.A. Perceptions of clients by professional helpers. *Psychological Bulletin,* 1978, *85,* 968-1000.

Yalom, I.D. *The theory and practice of group psychotherapy.* New York: Basic Books, 1975.

Youngren, M.A. *The functional relationship of depression and problematic interpersonal behavior.* Unpublished doctoral dissertation, University of Oregon, 1978.

Youngren, M.A., & Lewinsohn, P.M. The functional relation between depression and problematic interpersonal behavior. *Journal of Abnormal Psychology,* 1980, *89,* 333-341.

Zeiss, A.M. Interpersonal behavior problems of the depressed: A study of outpatient treatment. *Dissertation Abstracts International,* 1977, *38,* 28950-28956B (University Microfilm No. 77, 27, 205).

Zeiss, A.M., Lewinsohn, P.M., & Muñoz, R.F. Nonspecific improvement effects in depression using interpersonal, cognitive, and pleasant events focused treatments. *Journal of Consulting and Clinical Psychology,* 1979, *47,* 427-439.

Zung, W.W.K. A self-rating depression scale. *Archives of General Psychiatry,* 1965, *12,* 63-70.